CHARLOTTE MASON MADE EASY

DISCLAIMER AND/OR LEGAL NOTICES:

The author of this book has attempted to make the information as accurate as possible. However, the information in this book is for personal educational use only and is provided in good faith without any express or implied warranty. The author has provided book titles as a service to readers. This service does not mean that the author wholeheartedly endorses those books any way.

This edition published in 2020 by
Living Book Press
www.livingbookpress.com

ISBN: 978-1-922348-24-1

© 2020 Stephanie Walmsley

All rights reserved. No part of this publication may be reproduced, stored in a retrieval system, or transmitted in any other form or means – electronic, mechanical, photocopying, recording or otherwise, without the prior permission of the copyright owner and the publisher or as provided by Australian law.

 A catalogue record for this book is available from the National Library of Australia

charlotte mason
MADE
EASY

How to read Charlotte Mason's work and apply her philosophy in 12 easy lessons.

www.CharlotteMasonMadeEasy.com

CONTENTS

	INTRODUCTION	1
1.	MEET CHARLOTTE MASON	3
2.	SHORT LESSONS AND A TIMETABLE	20
3.	LEARNING ABOUT IDEAS	32
4.	LIVING BOOKS	41
5.	DOWN WITH TWADDLE!	49
6.	NARRATION	61
7.	OUTDOOR EDUCATION	72
8.	NATURE WALKS AND NATURE TABLES	83
9.	SCIENCE BOOKS	105
10.	ESTABLISHING GOOD HABITS	114
11.	HABITS – A CLOSER LOOK	127
12.	HISTORY: IS IT BORING AND DRY?	154
13.	FIVE TOOLS FOR TEACHING HISTORY	170
14.	HOW TO MAKE YOUR OWN TIMELINE	185
	A LAST WORD	189
	ABOUT THE AUTHOR	190

INTRODUCTION

You have in your hands a book which is the result of my own personal experience over many years of using Charlotte Mason's philosophies to teach and tutor children and to guide and teach parents about Charlotte Mason.

Over the years I have discovered that Charlotte Mason's own work is inaccessible to many modern readers because of its style and length. But relying on what others say Charlotte Mason said can leave too much room for 'interpretation'.

This book is a wonderful compromise; I am able to give you the benefit of my experience as a modern homeschooling mother, alongside carefully selected pages of Charlotte Mason's own work, so that you can read exactly what Charlotte wrote. And if you get a taste for her writing you can challenge yourself to buy or borrow the series of six volumes and read at greater length.

This is a very practical book, with ideas and suggestions coupled with Charlotte Mason's own work, and if you take careful note and read all Charlotte Mason's pages in this book you will learn about Charlotte Mason and her ideas, and you will gain confidence in what you want to do with your children.

In this book:
- I'll be introducing you to a notable teacher called Charlotte Mason.
- You'll learn about some of Miss Mason's philosophy including short lessons, how to make a timetable, narration, nature notebooks, teaching science, outdoor education, history, ideas, habits, and living books.
- You'll be given the opportunity to read Miss Mason's own words on these subjects and really gain an understanding of what she wanted to say.
- You'll have the opportunity and encouragement to apply what you are learning in your own family.

First I will introduce Charlotte Mason herself to you. And

then, starting at Chapter 2, I will show you how you can begin working with your children this week using Charlotte Mason's ideas.

Each chapter has a short introduction to an aspect of Charlotte Mason's philosophy. The idea is unpacked and discussed for you, and this is followed by an assignment. The assignment usually includes reading excerpts from Charlotte Mason's work. These excerpts are included in the supplementary readings following the chapter. This means that you can complete the assignments without having to purchase copies of Charlotte Mason's works.

I recommend reading a chapter a week, taking time to read carefully and to put each week's idea into practice.

CHAPTER 1.
MEET CHARLOTTE MASON

I am excited about introducing you to one of my heroines and helping you to see why I admire her so much.

I want to introduce you to Charlotte Mason the teacher. I want you to get a picture of her so that you can relate to her and have an understanding of the person behind the writing and the philosophy.

I want to make her 'come alive' to you, so that she is a real teacher and a real person in your imagination. This way, you can 'sit at her feet' to learn and really understand what she had to say about children and education.

WHO WAS CHARLOTTE MASON?

Charlotte Mason was born on 1 January 1842 in Bangor, North Wales. She was brought up in Liverpool and also spent time in the Isle of Man, which is a small independent island in the Irish Sea between England and Ireland. Her father was a businessman in the busy port city of Liverpool, and Charlotte was the only child of only children, so she had no extended family.

WRITING ABOUT HER CHILDHOOD, CHARLOTTE SAYS:

The first place I recollect was the Isle of Man, Douglas, I think, but I am not sure; we did not talk over things in our house. My mother was delicate and required sea air, so it happened that I was born in Bangor and that my earliest recollections are associated with the sea.

Drysalters were dealers in a range of chemical products, including glue, varnish, dye and colourings. They might supply salt or chemicals for preserving food and sometimes also sold pickles, dried meat or related items. The name *drysalter* or *dry-salter* was in use in the United Kingdom by the early 18th century when some drysalters concentrated on ingredients for producing dyes, and it was still current in the first part of the 20th century.

My father, J. H. Mason, was a Liverpool merchant, a 'drysalter,' and … a refined and simple man, very fond of books. The Liverpool house did not suit my mother, so we were seldom there. I had no brothers and sisters, and both parents were also only children, so I had no first cousins, and I think I was rather lonely as a child and got into the habit of not talking much.

I can recall only a few vignettes of our life in the Isle of Man, most of them, I fancy, belonging to my fifth year….

I remember my clothes quite well - a little ugly silk frock, which I somehow knew was one of my mother's dyed (so I suppose money was getting scarce), but to play on the beach this was covered with a holland overall, and there was a big flopping hat. Two little pelisses I remember, with little capes which were a joy to me; one was yellowy green and one was lavender, and the material was very soft; white frocks too, but I think they were too usual to be remembered….

I think I was a dull, silent, uninteresting and not very observant child; people used to like to pet me, perhaps because I was rather pretty. Anyway, my father used to say later that I was pretty as a child but grew plainer every day….

My mother wore long curls at each side of her face, and I can recall her coming to kiss me good night before going out in a low dress with a bertha and the curls tickling my face.

Bertha A wide, flat, round collar, often of lace or sheer fabric, worn with a low neckline in the Victorian era and resurrected in the 1940s.

There was a broad window-seat on a landing where my mother used to play with me at making dolls' houses, with lovely little snail-like shells that I have not seen elsewhere. I do not recollect any toys, but some beautifully made real fire-irons, which the little girl of the laundress gave me, and which my mother caused me to return, as they were rather valuable.

Pat-a-cake, pat-a-cake, baker's man must belong to an earlier age, but I remember my glee when my mother got to 'Mark it with P and put in the oven for Popsey and me.' But later some lady friend said such a great girl should not be called Popsey, but by her proper name, so I was Charlotte henceforth."

(Pages 1 and 2. The Story of Charlotte Mason by Essex Cholmondley (pronounced, "Chumly"))

I think this gives us such a vivid picture of the 'little girl', Charlotte, doesn't it? I can really see her mother with the curls, and the little dresses that Charlotte was wearing.

LET'S HEAR MORE ABOUT HER CHILDHOOD…

… On account of my mother's delicacy we used to live a great deal in the Isle of Man, which was within easy reach of Liverpool, and one or two recollections of those quite early days have been of great use to me. One day my mother was lying down and reading, and with the idle curiosity of a child of four or five I asked what she was reading. She looked up with a smile and said 'Pope's Homer's Odyssey' in the way in which we give answers to children which it amuses us to know how little they will understand. I think the subject was never referred to again, but I found out then, though my mother did not tell me any tales of Ulysses, that strange names offer no difficulties to children, and today I know that small children in elementary schools will talk glibly of Nausicaa, Telemachus, Agamemnon; that in fact they never turn a hair at the most difficult names associated with interesting ideas.

One other memory I got from seaside life which has affected my general trend of thought. I was being bathed from the shore one day, and somehow my father fell and I was dropped in. My mother was swimming at a distance and swam to the spot where no doubt I was all right by then, but the beauty and desirableness of swimming and all athletic exercises have influenced my thoughts of education.

The years '48 and '49 proved disastrous for my father, as for many another, and for some years we lived in small furnished lodgings. But all the time my parents read, and the first book I remember as a book was the big volume of Layard's Nineveh. The text was nothing to me, but the strange, monstrous pictures opened a new world, a sort of Milky Way of knowledge, and I think this little incident has led me to the conclusion that the whole field of knowledge should, as far as is any way possible, be opened to children.

Gifts were few in our family of three because for years we were very poor, but my eighth birthday brought me a gift of Robinson Crusoe. Meantime my parents, who were glad of the occupation, educated me (with some lessons from outside), father taking some subjects, my mother others...

But about this time came my vocation. ... [One day I saw] a tall lady with a dark shawl thrown scarfwise across her shoulders, a bonnet whose black strings floated, and a whole train of tiny children holding on to her skirts and following her.... this was the mistress of a girls' school near by.

The idea did not take shape at the time, but somehow I knew that teaching was the thing to do, and above all the teaching of poor children like those I had been watching. We got to know this lady. I found that her graceful appearance did not belie her. She took me to her school now and then, and I sat beside her on what was called a monitor's box and was all ears for the teaching of the great girls. And then came to me another fertile idea. The girls of the first class ranged between fifteen and seventeen, I should think, girls who would now be doing great things at a high school. They belonged to the professional classes, girls who wore watches and, sometimes, rings, and who read English history out of a miserable little book a quarter of an inch thick and entirely uninteresting.

I found out from that lesson how necessary it is that children should have books, good books, considerable and well-written books, for notwithstanding Butters we read books at home and at the time I was reading the Waverley novels. How our friend contrived to get the little children about her I never found out, but probably they were attracted as I was.

Charlotte's father suffered heavy financial losses in his business while Charlotte was growing up. Following this financial crisis, his wife died in 1858. Mr Mason never recovered from his wife's death and he died soon afterwards, leaving Charlotte a penniless orphan at the tender age of sixteen.

This detailed background to Charlotte's early life helps us to understand her vocation and passion, which was teaching and children.

EARLY ADULTHOOD

Charlotte stayed with friends until she was 18, when she went to a teacher training college for a year.

In 1864, Charlotte was photographed during her first visit to the village of Ambleside in the English Lake District. She was twenty-two. Her friend described her like this: *'Her hair was of the darkest shade of brown, almost black. Her eyes were blue-grey, her height five feet four inches.*

Charlotte began teaching in Worthing on the south coast of England. Under her management the school became very well known in the neighbourhood. It is said that *'perfect order was maintained without any severity and the pupils worked with intelligence and eagerness'.* No wonder Miss Mason made many friends in Worthing and was recognized as an authority on education. She taught there for 12 years before moving to Chichester where she was a lecturer for four years.

BRADFORD

In 1880, when Charlotte was in her late thirties, she moved to Bradford in the north of England to teach in a school kept by one of her friends and also to get some time for writing about education. In Bradford she gave a series of lectures to ladies on "Home Education". These lectures were so popular that they were published under the title of 'Home Education', which is the first volume in Charlotte Mason's 'Original Home School Series'.

Although Charlotte didn't enjoy very good health, she had a lot of friends and travelled to Continental Europe most years. She liked walking, and nature, and wrote geography books for children. She joined clubs and societies and visited her friends around the country. It's said that she was an inspiration to everyone she met, and she was certainly very popular and well loved.

MOVING TO AMBLESIDE

In 1891, when Charlotte Mason was nearly fifty, she realised a long ambition and was able to move to the small Lake District village of Ambleside, where she founded a college of education which she called "The House of Education".

We have first hand accounts of people who met and knew Charlotte. They always speak with respect and affection about her. And for me, this is inspirational because Charlotte Mason the teacher becomes a heroine to me, as much for the way in which she conducted her life, as for her teaching methods.

In 1894 Charlotte Mason was able to acquire a large Georgian house called Scale How. This was to be the hub of the college and remained so until recent times.

Scale How in the 1890s

THE TIMES SHE LIVED IN

Charlotte Mason lived in a time of great change, spanning the nineteenth and twentieth centuries. It was a time of Communism, Fascism, Darwinism, Eugenics, Determinism. (Lots of *isms*)

It was a time of Van Gogh, Impressionism, Post Impressionism and the Pre-Raphaelite brotherhood in art; Romanticism and Gilbert and Sullivan in music; Thomas Carlyle and John Ruskin in writing.

It was a time of Freud, Montessori, John Ruskin, Rudolph Steiner who started Waldorf schools and the expansion of philosophy and psychology...

There was lots of discussion about the role of 'nature versus nurture' in how a child grew and developed. Some people believed that 'nature' ruled all. That is to say that a child was born good or bad and no amount of upbringing could change the character or personality of a child. To see this played out, just consider the story of "Oliver Twist" by Dickens, written in 1838. In the story, the little boy, Oliver, is of noble birth, and no amount of temptation or training will persuade the child to do evil things.

Others believed that 'nurture' ruled and that upbringing was everything. Just because a child had wicked parents, didn't mean that the child was destined to a life of wickedness too. And, in fact, that the right upbringing could guarantee a certain result.

Charlotte Mason addressed this very issue in a unique way. She said that each child is born with the possibility of good

A photograph of Scale How taken in recent times by Stephanie

Charlotte Mason in 1920

and evil in him. That we need to train a child to make good choices.

She also talked about treating children as people, short lessons, narration, habits, nature journals, living books, and ideas. These are the main topics that Charlotte Mason is remembered for today.

LATER YEARS

Charlotte Mason spent the rest of her life in Ambleside. She died in January 1923.

VISITING AMBLESIDE TODAY

I grew up about 50 miles (80 km) from Ambleside and have made countless visits there over the years. Ambleside today is a small Lakeland town with narrow streets, stone buildings, slate roofs, and plenty of tourist shops. The house, Scale How is still there; out of the town, on the road to Rydal Water. And until very recently, it was still a place of learning.

On my last visit to Ambleside, I visited Scale How and Charlotte Mason's grave. The inscription on her grave is very moving, and quite long. It seems very tender to me. It reads:

"In loving memory of Charlotte Maria Shaw Mason, Born Jan 1 1842, died Jan 16 1923, Thine eyes shall see the King in His beauty. Founder of the Parents National Educational Union, The Parents Union School and The

House of Education. She devoted her life to the work of education, believing that children are dear to our heavenly Father, and that they are a precious national possession. Education is an atmosphere, a discipline, a life. I am, I can, I ought, I will. For the children's sake."

PEOPLE WHO KNEW CHARLOTTE MASON TELL US ABOUT HER

What follows are some reflections about Charlotte Mason from people who knew her. They will help to enrich your understanding of who Charlotte Mason was. Hopefully, you might even start to view her as a beloved teacher to you.

From Violet Parker, one of the first students at the House of Education: (from The Story of Charlotte Mason by Essex Cholmondley. pp 37-38)

My first recollection of Miss Mason was in January 1889 when my mother and I were invited to meet her at the vicarage, Forest Gate. Our friends the Rev. Edward and Mrs Wynne had lately moved from Manningham, Bradford, and Mrs Wynne had told us how Miss Mason, in order to raise needed funds for their church there, had given a series of talks on educational matters. These had appeared in book form as Home Education. A year or two later the 'House of Education' was opened. Three other girls and myself were the first students.

How well I remember that night of 15th January 1892. A cold but lovely drive by coach from Windermere to Ambleside: trees heavily laden with snow on one hand-a black lake on the other, a mysterious and wonderful fairyland to our delighted eyes. At the end of our journey-on arrival at Ambleside there was a warm welcome from Miss Mason who so soon won our hearts. Whatever our surroundings might have been, we should have been happy merely to be with her!

We were at Fairfield House for three months, then when Springfield became vacant either Miss Mason or my mother took it....

My mother furnished it and managed it for some time until she found it too much for her; then Miss Mason bought the furniture and my mother moved to Walton Cottage.

At Springfield Miss Mason's room was the large one at the top of the stairs on the right. I loved being there and so enjoyed the yellow poppies which came up everywhere. It was such a pretty walk over the stile across the fields to church. Miss Mason took Miss Beale that way. Dr Schofield also visited her there.... In those days Miss Mason devoted nearly all her time to us and we spent our mornings with her at Mr Fleming's Lecture Room 1 in the village where were excellent classrooms for our purpose; she was able to go for walks with us or for excursions by road or lake. I well remember when she came for a row with us. She usually went with us to Mrs Firth's weekly 'picture talk'- so much appreciated. How we delighted in everything, but Miss Mason was far from strong and often greatly overtaxed herself for the work's sake. Upon more than one occasion she had to fight serious illness but I cannot remember her ever referring to herself.

As I look back what impresses me most about Miss Mason was, I think, her extraordinary power of getting the best out of everybody and of making 'the lion lie down with the lamb.' She seemed by some magic to eliminate causes of discord, but these seldom occurred in the atmosphere of peace and content which she created. By her presentation of the good, that which was bad and ugly simply ceased to exist. I think Miss Mason's outstanding quality was her intuitive understanding . . . she was often almost uncanny in her ' judgment of character.... But her humility (in spite of her power), combined with her urgent desire for the person's good, brought out the best in those who were associated with her.

Here are a few quotations taken from a book of collected writings about Charlotte Mason. The book is called, "In Memoriam". It is out of copyright and you can read and download the whole book here: http://www.archive.org/details/inmemoriamcharlo00pareuoft

From the Times Educational Supplement January 20 1923
A Personal Tribute

A correspondent writes:—Charlotte Mason was that rare combination, an original thinker and philosopher and at the same time, a wonderful organiser and business woman. She was wise and witty, keenly interested in the things of the world, birds and flowers, books and people, but with an inner vision *for the beyond, and the graciousness of manner and selfless consideration for others which marked the grande dame of a passing age. She treated the smallest child with courtesy. She was gracious to the youngest member of her household just as she was to the great of the land who were among her disciples. Her students and all who came under her influence caught the fire of her enthusiasm for her educational principles together with her single-mindedness and humility.*

She never allowed her methods of teaching and philosophy of education to be called by her name, but by that of the society she founded to spread them. Thus her work will continue and be ably carried on by those she has trained and appointed for the task. She was at work up to four days before her death, and personally superintended the many arrangements for accommodating the ever-increasing number of students wishing to enter her college. Her end was the passing of a great spirit. With all her powers of mind and heart fresh and keen, memory and apprehension unimpaired, she fell asleep after many days spent for the good of humanity. Her teaching has spread to almost every part of the globe; the pupils of her correspondence school are to be found in home schoolrooms, in private and council schools, and many generations of happy children filled with the joy of living and of learning will rise up and call her blessed.

From I.B.S. Whitaker Thompson.

...I resolved to seek the earliest opportunity of making Miss Mason's acquaintance and this fortunately happened in the autumn of [1887]. She was staying at Highfield, Ilkley, a house which was a favourite resort for intellectual and poetic natures in holiday time, high up on the edge of the moor, and as I was in the neighbourhood I ventured to write and ask her to allow me to go over one afternoon, and met with her usual kind response. Accordingly I climbed up from the station at Ben Rhydding one hot August day and there in the sunshine and the heather I spent a happy and memorable hour with the sweet and gentle person for whom I had acquired such an inward respect and veneration.

Her encouraging manner and quiet simple talk disarmed all nervousness and made me entirely at ease; her understanding and sympathy, her love of children and confidence in the good in them, her ideas of developing their tastes and talents, of avoiding the stumbling blocks put in their way by injudicious elders, her respect for the efforts of well-meaning parents ignorant of their own inefficiency, and her earnest desire to help them, her estimate of the value of early environment, example and training, the formation of habits, the love of Nature, the freedom of leisure, the atmosphere of truth that should surround these tender little ones whom none may despise, the ultimate goal of character, all these and many other ideals inspired me with noble ambitions, though with a despairing sense of shortcoming; for what mother could suffice for these things? Later glimpses, all too short, but always a privilege, came in meetings at Bad Nauheim, where the grave heart trouble that affected her for so many years, caused her to spend several weeks each summer following the cure, which happily brought invariable benefit. The wonderful patience and cheerfulness with which she bore her physical frailty and limitations were a living testimony to that Faith which was her 'sure foundation' and inspired the optimism and calmness of spirit, the wise and steadfast philosophy that made her such an unfailing counsellor to others in difficult ways, and gave pause to realise she tapped the Source that makes "quietness and confidence your strength."

A Few Recollections by Helen Webb.

It was at a drawing-room meeting at the London house of the Duchess of Portland, in the year 1892, that I first met Miss Mason and heard her speak. I have always remembered the impression then made up on me by her gracious personality, and great charm of voice and manner.

The title of the address is forgotten, but it concerned her gospel of education and from that day others, besides myself, must have realised that they had seen a new vision. That was the beginning too of a friendship which has been for 30 years one of the greatest privileges and pleasures of my life.

A little later in Florence I came upon Miss Mason and her friend, Mrs. Firth, standing by Giotto's Tower, and together we studied his beautiful medallions. I shall always especially associate with them that of the woman weaving on the loom which Ruskin copied when he revived hand-weaving in the Lake country.

In September 1894 I paid my first never-to-be-forgotten visit to Miss Mason at Ambleside. ... The day after my arrival Miss Mason took me across the road to view the big house on the hill which she thought of moving into, so as to have all her students under one roof, and make a worthy home for the House of Education. As we walked up the drive the sun shone brightly, and in front of the house we stopped and turned round to gaze on Loughrigg and Wansfell, with Windermere between and said to each other, "Just think, Wordsworth stood here and looked at all that!" for his niece Mrs. Harrison (nee Wordsworth) had lived at Scale How in his life-time and till 1892. We went all over the house, up and down and into every corner, and decided with Mr. Curwen, the architect, who met us there, about the few alterations and improvements which would be needed. Altogether we planned for a beautiful future, nearly 29 years of which, with its fine record, now belong to the past.

Another day Miss Mason took me to Keswick on the top of the mail coach. It was a good old fashioned coach with four horses, a leisurely vehicle from which one had plenty of time to see everything. That day I had a wonderful lesson in "sight-seeing," as Miss Mason understood it. And what delightful fun we had, and how much enjoyment out of all kinds of little everyday trifles!

Shortly after this time when Miss Mason had to realise the physical limitations due to ill-health, she had the great wisdom to order her life in such a way that every available grain of energy could be given to the work which was so dear to her, so that in the many future visits which I paid to her our excursions did not go beyond the beautiful daily drives in the near neighbourhood.

These were taken in her little Victoria, driven by her faithful man Barrow. Here we looked for red-starts, and there to see if the daffodils were in flower, and some days we went round by Grasmere and bought ginger-bread from old Sarah Nelson.

I wish I could give a clearer picture of it all. Those who were at that delightful Conference at Ambleside last May will always carry with them some idea of the charm of Scale How under its dear Mistress.

Miss Mason's Love of the Country Drives by T. H. Barrow (Coachman)

Having served my late dear Mistress for 24 years, I should like to make known her love of, and interest in, all that moved or grew along the lanes or moors, for it was Miss Mason's delight to seek the quiet lanes and bits of moor away from the noisy motors, and only quite recently, using her own words, have they begun "to poach on our private drives."

From 1898 for a good many years Miss Mason would take the tea-basket on her drive, when with the late Miss Armitt, or the Hon. Mrs. Franklin or others. If the weather was hot, in the woods by the lake towards the ferry; if cool Miss Mason enjoyed the hillside between Chapel Stile and High Close, where unrivalled views could be obtained of river, lake and mountain.

We could take at least twenty different drives, or circles, very rarely covering the same road on return except for a little distance from home. Each drive had its own peculiar charm. In September, the autumn tints were best on one. In October, another would be more brilliant. Then November brought the bracken on the mountains to the warm russet colour, Miss Mason's delight. A cold blast in December brought the Redwing to their favourite haunts for shelter, and then we knew a storm was brewing. In December, January and February, we usually saw the different species of wild duck on Elterwater, Loughrigg Tarn, or Rydal Water. The end of February and early March saw the Wild Goose going back to the breeding ground on the Scottish coast. Barngates being a favourite crossing place for them. It was on this drive in 1920 Miss Mason saw a pair of Waxwings quite close at hand and on a former occasion three Redpolls. Towards the latter end of March we saw the Curlew by Barngates come to look up his nesting ground. April brought Redstart and Wheatear. Though small birds, Miss Mason's watchful eye seldom missed them even in 1922.

Each drive seemed to yield something of its own. One snug corner produced Hazel Blossom, another Coltsfoot flowers; some drives were profuse in Wild Roses and Honeysuckle; another in Bog Bean and Bog Myrtle' another in Grass of Parnassus; and even the small Milkwort did not escape Miss Mason's keen eye.

Very often did we follow nature's ways in evading the storm. Sometimes, when quite calm at "The House of Education," (sheltered from North and East winds) on reaching the open we found a boisterous wind and it was then we had to follow the cunning of the fox and hug the sheltered side of Loughrigg to

Selfish Bridge, thence to Barngates, and with back to wind could get our little circular drive without discomfort.

Miss Mason was fond of her horse, which was a great help in getting close to birds as they don't fear animals so much as persons. And it was always her first enquiry when staying at hotels during Easter Holidays,—Had I and her favourite little mare Duchess, been made comfortable and well fed? To her friends who asked why she did not have a motor, her answer was,—"I can talk to a horse but not to a motor." To illustrate her contention that it was so, I very well remember when once by Shelwith Falls on a stormy day, Miss Mason wished to return, not feeling well, and she had given me the word to turn again for home. Through the rush of water I had not heard Miss Mason's words, but Duchess had, and when I attempted to restrain her from turning, Miss Mason said it was quite right, Duchess had heard and knew all about it.

Miss Mason's nerve during these later years was marvellous, for we encountered all kinds of motorists, reckless and otherwise. We have even had horse's feet on the motor bonnet. Still she kept calm where many a younger person would have been panic-stricken and probably by leaping out would have caused serious harm to herself.

Miss Mason was always punctual, never kept man and horse waiting and never left her carriage without the kindly, 'Good afternoon' and 'Thank you, Barrow.' And (had our drive been prolific in birds, &c.,) "We've had a splendid bag." And I am proud of having had the honour and pleasure, for it was a pleasure, of driving such a kind and noble lady whose like none can excel.

And her end was Peace.

From H. E. Wix. Ex-Student, House of Education.

Perhaps there never has lived anyone who more speedily and lastingly won the friendship of persons she never saw. Teachers who had only known of her for a few months felt the blank of her loss with a curious intensity; so did parents whose knowledge of her was confined to gratitude for her teaching in Home Education and Parents and Children..

...Breadth and balance are perhaps the main marks of Miss

Mason's teaching, so that there are many standpoints from which we may try to study it. Surely few educationists have solved both a theory and a philosophy of education—in its broadest sense—and a practical concrete method of teaching as well. There are these two main sides of her ideal, often separated but not really separable. First, the upbringing of the child, the person; the teaching habit, the training of the will, the gradual evolution of character. Founded on this and on much more, is Miss Mason's theory and practice of education in its narrower sense; how to teach children in their school days.

MY OWN EXPERIENCE OF TEACHING THE CHARLOTTE MASON WAY

I first heard of Charlotte Mason when I was training to be a teacher, many years ago in England. At that time, she was one of a long list of educators we learnt about. And I recognised that I myself had been taught with some of her methods.

I next heard of Charlotte Mason in 1990 when Karen Andreola started publishing her *Parents' Review* magazines. I devoured the journals each quarter and got my own set of *Charlotte Mason's Original Homeschool* Series.

Not many homeschoolers had heard of the name of Charlotte Mason at that time, and to begin with, many equated the name with 'teatime', classical music, picture study and poetry. Some people even had special tea parties with classical music blaring, while they drank tea and read poetry. Obviously a rather silly response to a lot of good ideas. Nowadays I would hope that most of us would be more sensible and enjoy all aspects of a rich, broad education in a measured manner.

As people started to read more carefully and built up an understanding of the depth of Charlotte Mason's work and ideas, so too, did the quality of teaching and discussion improve.

Today a lot of people have heard of Charlotte Mason, and there is a range of top-notch support for those of us who want to follow through in more depth.

The first introduction to Charlotte Mason is usually hearing talk about good books, narration and nature study, but things do go much deeper than that. You will have already seen that Charlotte Mason didn't suggest a narrow curriculum at all. On the contrary, she taught and recommended a very wide curriculum. It's the sort of teaching and learning which lends itself beautifully to homeschooling.

In my own family I have discovered that using Charlotte Mason's ideas can produce a rich and happy lifestyle of learning that can be applied as much or as little as you like.

So many times I have heard of people wanting to apply Charlotte Mason's philosophies, but they are unsure of where to start, or they have tried and had difficulties, or they have got so far, but without success.

I would like to share more about Charlotte Mason's methods and philosophies of education with you, and I invite you to join me in learning, step by step, how to teach your children, using Charlotte Mason's wonderful ideas and methods.

Stephanie at the front door of Scale How

CHAPTER 2.
SHORT LESSONS AND A TIMETABLE

One of the biggest problems many people have when they first start considering Charlotte Mason's philosophy for their homeschool is the sheer number of different subjects that Charlotte Mason talks about. People wonder how they can fit all the subjects into their timetable.

Well, I am about to let you into a secret. It's not hard. There are two reasons why it's not hard.

- First of all, you don't teach all the subjects to the children at every age and stage (more of this in a minute).
- And secondly, Charlotte Mason suggested short lessons. If you have short lessons you can fit more subjects into the day.

What did Charlotte Mason say about lesson times? She gave really helpful and quite precise information here.

… the lessons are short, seldom more than twenty minutes in length for children under eight; and this, for two or three reasons. The sense that there is not much time for his sums or his reading, keeps the child's wits on the alert and helps to fix his attention; he has time to learn just so much of any one subject as it is good for him to take in at once: and if the lessons be judiciously alternated—sums first, say, while the brain is quite fresh; then writing, or reading—some more or less mechanical exercise, by way of a rest; and so on, the program varying a little from day to day, but the same principle throughout—a 'thinking' lesson first, and a 'painstaking' lesson to follow,—the child gets through his morning lessons without any sign of weariness.

Ahhhh! This sounds so simple!

Have you ever had a dawdler? Don't worry, most of us have had at least one dawdler for long enough to make us not forget! Try what Charlotte Mason suggests in the passage above. It helps.

And if you are still having trouble, then watch out for what is coming up in Chapter Three, which might inspire you to inspire your child to work at a steady pace and give up dawdling.

Now, let's look at what subjects to teach and how to make a timetable.

1. WHAT SUBJECTS?

Let me show you how to make a list of subjects you want to teach your child and then I will show you how to fit the subjects into the timetable.

We will start with the basics: English and mathematics. Everyone will want to teach these subjects. They will go on your timetable four or five times a week, no matter what age your homeschooled child. But here's the big secret; the first reason I mentioned earlier of why it's not hard. You don't teach every subject at once to all age ranges.

Let's unpack this a bit more. First, I'll make a list of subjects. Some of them you might have heard mentioned when people are specifically referring to 'Charlotte Mason'.

- Reading
- Spelling
- Grammar
- Writing
- Dictation
- Copy work
- Shakespeare
- Poetry
- Composition
- Mathematics
- Science
- History
- Geography
- Art
- Foreign languages
- Picture study
- Music
- Music appreciation
- Outdoor education
- Physical education
- Technology

And that doesn't include any time spent reading aloud to your child or listening to narration if you are working with younger children. Or having planning meetings and reading your child's work if you are working with older children.

Phew! No wonder the timetable feels crowded and you feel overwhelmed and inadequate!

But wait a minute! Let's take another look at that list of subjects.

The first nine 'subjects' on the list can come under the heading of 'English'.

And when you are teaching English, you will only teach a few from that long list of topics, and what you teach will depend on the age of your child. Here's the list of English topics, broken down into age-appropriate levels.

1. Pre-reading, you will be allowing time for your child to do lots of physical activities. (We'll cover that in more detail in Chapter Six.)

2. Emergent reading, you will be concentrating on teaching your child the alphabet, phonics and letter formation. The child will be copying your writing or writing over the top of your letters or dotted letters.

3. Almost fluent reading, this child will be doing some copy work and spelling. He will do each one three or four times a week for a short time.

4. Fluent reader who is fine-tuning his writing skills. This child should have good handwriting now, but he will be working on grammar and starting dictation. The dictation will ensure he gets good handwriting practice, and it will help you to see that the spelling is in place. He will be introduced to Shakespeare and poetry in a happy, relaxed way. Take a month or two for poetry and then a month or two for Shakespeare.

5. Pre-teen child who is a fluent reader and writer. This child will be working on composition and will be starting on written narrations (more on this in Chapter Six). He will be studying Shakespeare and poetry too.

6. Teen homeschooler, this child is working semi independently, producing beautiful written narrations and compositions, as well as analysing work and reading classic literature.

As you can see, the child will not be covering everything all the time. So, although a child will eventually cover all topics, it's spread out over several years. And at any stage, he is only covering two or three aspects from this long list.

A VERY IMPORTANT TRUTH

What I have to say now is really important. Read it more than once and try and get the message into your heart so that you won't be distracted or discouraged on those difficult days.

- It's good to have an attitude of seeing your child's education in terms of years, rather than in terms of 'today', 'this week', or even 'this year'.
- It's good to think of it in terms of a lifestyle of learning.
- And it helps to keep focused more long distance, on the direction which you are heading, towards your long-term goal.

WHY PEOPLE FAIL IN HOMESCHOOLING

One big reason people fail in homeschooling, no matter what method they use, is that they try to fit a whole childhood of education into a few weeks or months, and they exhaust themselves worrying about what they are not doing and trying to do it all at once.

Another reason for failure is that homeschooling parents jump from one 'method' to another, from one curriculum to another, all the time trying to find the best one. They hear about new ideas they think it might be a good idea to try and incorporate 'the best' of everything into their homeschooling lifestyle.

ANOTHER IMPORTANT TRUTH

Here's another very important truth for you: you can't do it all.

You can't, and if you try you will suffer from 'overwhelm' and 'burnout'.

Now here's what you do when overwhelm threatens you. You remember that Charlotte Mason education is NOT complicated; it's SIMPLE.

And you revert to your timetable. Your timetable will keep you focused and hold back the 'overwhelm'. So, let's work on a timetable.

2. THE TIMETABLE

Have you noticed how children like to have a clear idea of what is expected of them and what is coming next? I know this is true in my own family. One question the children would ask me every morning when we got up was, "What are we doing today?"

I answered the question patiently, but it confused me for a very long time. Why did they ask? We had a timetable, after all. Then I realised that they weren't looking at the timetable, so they didn't know what was coming. And anyway, I sometimes wandered off the timetable.

So I got more serious about trying to stick to the timetable (within limits of kindness and flexibility) and I put a copy of the timetable on the wall, and not just in my diary. That solved the problem! The children knew where they stood, and they could see at a glance what was coming up next.

Here's what Charlotte Mason has to say about a timetable:

...let us look in at a home schoolroom managed on sound principles. In the first place, there is a time-table, written out fairly, so that the child knows what he has to do and how long each lesson is to last. This idea of definite work to be finished in a given time is valuable to the child, not only as training him in habits of order, but in diligence; he learns that one time is not 'as good as another'; that there is no right time left for what is not done in its own time; and this knowledge alone does a great deal to secure the child's attention to his work.

That's pretty clear to me, and it's also what I have found to be effective with my own children.

WORKING OUT A TIMETABLE

We will work out a timetable that you can expect to have in place for about three to six months, depending on the age of your children. The younger the children the more frequently you will change your timetable as the children change and grow.

Also, the newer you are to homeschooling and making or keeping to a timetable, the more frequently you will need to make adjustments to the timetable. Until you get it just right for you. One of your biggest problems will be that you will probably want to try and fit in too much. So make sure you leave 'breathing space' in the day and don't be tempted to fill in every minute with activities.

Here's ten easy steps to working out your timetable:

1. First make a list of subjects you want to cover over the next few months with your child. Try to look at what your child needs, rather than what you think they might be covering in school, or what you think other people might be covering with their children.

2. Decide what times of the day are best for you and the children to do work sitting at the table. What we might call 'seat work'.

3. Make a list of other subjects and events in your week that need to be taken into consideration.

4. Print several copies of the blank timetable found at http://charlottemasonmadeeasy.com/bookbonus

5. We are going to assume that your child is pre-teen, so that you are working out his timetable for him (teens will have some say in how they plan their weekly studies, fitting in with the family commitments). So now, write into your timetable all the things that are fixed. This will include clubs that the children belong to, lessons outside the home, doctor or medical therapy sessions that are ongoing, church activities which take place during the week, etc.

6. Write down your family's breakfast and morning routine times. Add your family's lunch time and dinner time.

7. Now you are ready to add mathematics and English. Put these on the timetable every day. Try to aim for a similar time each day. For a young child, under ten, make the lessons short. Make the writing times anywhere between ten and thirty minutes, according to age and ability. Slot in the subjects according to ability and according to the list on pages nine and ten.

8. After adding mathematics and English you can add science. Like English, this will include a variety of topics like outdoor education and nature study. (More of this in a future chapter.) You will have a couple of short lessons a week.

9. Now add the rest of the subjects. Some subjects will happen just once or twice a week – art, picture study, history, geography, music appreciation. Some subjects will be a short lesson every day. – foreign languages, music.
10. In the afternoons, leave time for play, crafts and hobbies.

That's it. By following these ten steps you will soon have a workable timetable which includes all the Charlotte Mason lessons you want. Remember to include HEAPS of 'breathing space' in your day; otherwise you will be miserable, trying to keep to a difficult timetable.

YOUR SECRET WEAPON

And now here's an important secret weapon to help this timetable work for you. When you next check your emails and someone has a new idea for a new system or an academic subject which you haven't included in your timetable, you RESIST the temptation to try and add another subject.

Instead, you write it on a page in your diary, which is entitled "Ideas for the future". Then in six months or more, when you are ready to make a new timetable, you can look at the "Ideas for the future" list and see if any of the things in your list still appeal and/or are suitable for your family. If they are you can add them to your timetable, using the steps that you've learnt here.

SUMMARY

In this chapter:
- I have shown you ten steps to making a workable timetable.
- I've shown you how simple it is to fit in a wide variety of subjects.
- I've given you a secret weapon to protect you and your timetable from failure.

ASSIGNMENT

This chapter's assignment is pretty straightforward.

- Start thinking about your timetable. If you are happy with your current timetable, use the 'ten steps' list to make a single change to your current timetable to make it even better. Otherwise, set aside time to have a big timetable overhaul.

- I recommend that you read the following pages of the SUPPLEMENT. This is your introduction to reading Charlotte Mason's own work.

- You might like to read a single chapter of this book each week; just choose a time in your week for *Charlotte Mason Made Easy,* and then read your chapter, make notes and write down your thoughts and plans. This will really help you as we consider some of the ideas and philosophies of Charlotte Mason together.

SUPPLEMENT

I have a very brief introduction to *Charlotte Mason's Original Homeschool Series* for you. We will start near the beginning of the first volume, which is called *Home Education*. This is interesting for us to read because Charlotte Mason is talking about the importance of mothers in a child's education, and we are assuming that it's a mother who is doing most of the home educating. I've picked out a couple of passages where Charlotte Mason talks about the importance of the mother in a child's education and how an educational system needs to fit a child without making the child into an idol.

Also, I have included a piece on how Charlotte Mason suggests you keep your timetable.

Volume 1, page 2

...it is upon the mothers of the present that the future of the world depends, in even a greater degree than upon the fathers, because it is the mothers who have the sole direction of the children's early, most impressible years. This is why we hear so frequently of great men who have had good mothers—that is, mothers who brought up their children themselves, and did not make over their gravest duty to indifferent persons.

"The mother is qualified," says Pestalozzi, "and qualified by the Creator Himself, to become the principal agent in the development of her child; ... and what is demanded of her is—a thinking love...God has given to the child all the faculties of our nature, but the grand point remains undecided—how shall this heart, this head, these hands be employed? to whose service shall they be dedicated? A question the answer to which involves a futurity of happiness or misery to a life so dear to thee. Maternal love is the first agent in education."

We are waking up to our duties, and in proportion, as mothers become more highly educated and efficient, they will doubtless feel the more strongly that the education of their children during the first six years of life is an undertaking hardly to be entrusted to any hands but their own. And they will take it up as their profession—that is, with the diligence, regularity, and punctuality which men bestow on their professional labours.

That the mother may know what she is about, may come thoroughly furnished to her work, she should have something more than a hearsay acquaintance with the theory of education, and with those conditions of the child's nature upon which such theory rests.

Volume 1, page 7

...That children should be trained to endure hardness, was a principle of the old regime. "I shall never make a sailor if I can't face the wind and rain," said a little fellow of five who was taken out on a bitter night to see a torchlight procession; and, though, shaking with cold, he declined the shelter of a shed. Nowadays, the shed is everything; the children must not be permitted to suffer from fatigue or exposure.

That children should do as they are bid, mind their books, and take pleasure as it offers when nothing stands in the way, sums up the old theory; now, the pleasures of children are apt to be made more account than their duties.

Formerly, they were brought up in subjection; now, the elders give place, and the world is made for the children.

English people rarely go so far as the parents of that story in French Home Life, who arrived an hour late at a dinner party, because they had been desired by their girl of three to undress and go to bed when she did, and were able to steal away only when the child was asleep. We do not go so far, but that is the direction in which we are now moving; and how far the new theories of education are wise and humane, the outcome of more widely spread physiological and psychological knowledge, and how far they just pander to child worship to which we are all succumbing, is not a question to be decided off hand....

Volume 1, page 9

...If a human being were a machine, education could do no more for him than to set him in action in prescribed ways, and the work of the educator would be simply to adopt a good working system or set of systems.

But the educator has to deal with a self-acting, self-developing being, and his business is to guide, and assist in, the production of the latent good in that being, the dissipation of the latent evil, the preparation of the child to take his place in the world at his best, with every capacity for good that is in him developed into a power.

Volume 1, page 142

Time-table; Definite Work in a Given Time.—... let us look in at a home schoolroom managed on sound principles. In the first place, there is a time-table, written out fairly, so that the child knows what he has to do and how long each lesson is to last.

This idea of definite work to be finished in a given time is valuable to the child, not only as training him in habits of order, but in diligence; he learns that one time is not 'as good as another'; that there is no right time left for what is not done in its own time; and this knowledge alone does a great deal to secure the child's attention to his work.

Again, the lessons are short, seldom more than twenty minutes in length for children under eight; and this, for two or three reasons. The sense that there is not much time for his sums or his reading, keeps the child's wits on the alert and helps to fix his attention; he has time to learn just so much of any one subject as it is good for him to take in at once: and if the lessons be judiciously alternated—sums first, say, while the brain is quite fresh; then writing, or reading—some more or less mechanical exercise, by way of a rest; and so on, the program varying a little from day to day, but the same principle throughout—a 'thinking' lesson first, and a 'painstaking' lesson to follow,—the child gets through his morning lessons without any sign of weariness.

FAMILY HOMESCHOOL TIMETABLE

	Mon	Tue	Wed	Thur	Fri
Rise and early morning jobs					
Household organised by					
Morning session 1					
Break time					
Morning session 2					
Lunch and reading time					
Afternoon activities					
Pre-dinner jobs					
Dinner					
Evening activities, story times, bedtimes					
Adult time					

Download a copy of this timetable from
http://charlottemasonmadeeasy.com/bookbonus

CHAPTER 3.
LEARNING ABOUT IDEAS

Now that you have read some of Charlotte Mason's own work you will know just a little bit about the person and teacher I am referring to. It's important to have at least a small understanding of the person behind the theory. And this is why:

- Your understanding works like a torch on the theories, philosophies and methods you will come across as you read more and more of Charlotte Mason's work.
- You will understand better what Charlotte Mason was saying.
- You will have a clearer understanding of how to fit those philosophies and teachings into your own family.

In this chapter I'm going to talk to you about one of Charlotte Mason's passions – the thought that we need to feed children 'IDEAS'. She said that the life of the mind grows on ideas.

So we will look at ideas. Then you will have time to try clarifying some ideas for yourself.

WHAT IS AN IDEA?

An idea is anything which captivates our minds and causes us to think.

Ideas are usually imparted from one person to another through enthusiasm or conviction – which is where we get Charlotte Mason's term, "living book". Meaning that through the book, a "living thing of the mind" is passed on to the reader.

I like the things that Charlotte Mason had to say about ideas - how ideas behave, how they endure, how they pass from one mind to another.

Ideas can be good or bad, they can reproduce, and they can grow. They can have a powerful impact on people and change the way people behave.

Because we are spiritual beings, ideas have an impact on us that they would not have on animals who are primarily physical creatures.

WHAT DOES AN IDEA LOOK LIKE?

You can see ideas at work in the minds of even the smallest children:

- A baby grasps the idea that his fingers belong to him and he can control them.
- A one-year-old gets the idea that pushing the buttons on the remote makes all the adults in the room jump up and down and start yelling.
- A five-year-old gets the idea that the shape of "t" stands for a certain sound.
- You see your child wrestling with the idea of numbers reaching into infinity.
- You see your child considering the idea that blood is circulating though his body all the time, or that his heart beats all the time and when it stops he will die.
- Did you ever see that fabulous old movie, The Miracle Worker? Remember the famous scene when Helen Keller finally grasped the idea that words represented objects, beginning with the word "water"?

These are examples of ideas in action.

HOW POWERFUL ARE IDEAS?

Ideas have huge power in our lives. As well as inspiring us to action or experimentation, ideas can control our behaviour too.

For example,

- We absorb from our environment the idea that doing sloppy work is shameful, and work well done is something to be proud of.
- We get the idea that the world scorns a coward, but to be brave is noble.
- We believe the idea that hard work and diligence increase our chances of success.
- We get the idea that flossing and brushing our teeth is good for us.

Those kinds of ideas, planted in the mind, are the seeds that will, properly nourished, grow into the kinds of habits and character we want.

QUESTIONS

Now, some questions to ponder and respond to.

- What have you learnt about Charlotte Mason the person that has surprised you?
- Is there anything that you have learnt about Charlotte Mason's thoughts on ideas that has surprised you?
- What is an idea?
- Sometimes we find it hard to pin down exactly what is meant by "an idea"—can you think of some ideas that have taken root and blossomed in your children's lives?
- What about in your own life?

SUMMARY

In this chapter

- You have learnt some of what Charlotte Mason had to say about ideas.
- I have talked about what an idea is.
- I have described to you what an idea looks like.
- I have given you examples of ideas.
- And we considered the power of ideas in a person's life.

ASSIGNMENT

- Read what you can about IDEAS from The Original Homeschooling Series:
- Volume 1, pages 169 – 178 (pages 173 – 174 are in your supplement)
- Volume 2, pages 34 – 40 (also in your supplement)
- If you want to go deeper and are wondering what to read next, try these passages:
  - Volume 6 Introduction and Chapter I; pages 1 – 32
  - Volume 3 Chapters 17 – 19

SUPPLEMENT

HOME EDUCATION VOLUME 1 BY CHARLOTTE MASON

Pages 173 and 174

Children learn, to get Ideas.—The child must learn, in the second place, in order that ideas may be freely sown in the fruitful soil of his mind. 'Idea, the image or picture formed by the mind of anything external, whether sensible or spiritual.'—so, the dictionary; therefore, if the business of teaching be to furnish the child with ideas, any teaching which does not leave him possessed of a new mental image has, by so far, missed its mark.

Now, just think of the listless way in which the children too often drag through reading and tables, geography and sums, and you will see that it is a rare thing for any part of any lesson to flash upon them with the vividness which leaves a mental picture behind. It is not too much to say that a morning in which a child receives no new idea is a morning wasted, however closely the little student has been kept at his books.

Ideas Grow and Produce after their Kind.—For the dictionary appears to me to fall short of the truth in its definition of the term 'idea.' An idea is more than an image or picture; it is, so to speak, a spiritual germ endowed with vital force—with power, that is, to grow, and to produce after its kind.

It is the very nature of an idea to grow: as the vegetable germ secrets that it lives by, so, fairly implant an idea in the child's mind, and it will secrete its own food, grow, and bear fruit in the form of a succession of kindred ideas.

We know from our own experience that, let our attention be forcibly drawn to some public character, some startling theory, and for days after we are continually hearing or reading matter which bears on this one subject, just as if all the world were thinking about what occupies our thoughts: the fact being, that the new idea we have received is in the act of growth, and is reaching out after its appropriate food. This process of feeding goes on with peculiar avidity in childhood, and the growth of an idea in the child is proportionally rapid.

Scott and Stephenson worked with Ideas.—Scott got an idea, a whole group of ideas, out of the Border tales and ballads, the folklore of the country-side, on which his boyhood was nourished: his ideas grew and brought forth, and the Waverley novels are the fruit they bore. George Stephenson made little clay engines with his playmate, Thomas Tholoway; by-and-by, when he was an engineman, he was always watching his engine, cleaning it, studying it; an engine was his dominant idea, and it developed into no less a thing than the locomotive.

Value of Dominant Ideas.—But how does this theory of the vital and fruitful character of ideas bear upon the education of the child? In this way: give your a child a single valuable idea, and you have done more for his education than if you had laid upon his mind the burden of bushels of information; for the child who grows up with a few dominant ideas has his self-education provided for, his career marked out.

Lessons must furnish Ideas.—In order for the reception of an idea, the mind must be in an attitude of eager attention, and how to secure that state we have considered elsewhere.

One thing more: a single idea may be a possession so precious in itself, so fruitful, that the parent cannot fitly allow the child's selection of ideas to be a matter of chance; his lessons should furnish him with such ideas as shall make for his further education.

PARENTS AND CHILDREN VOLUME 2 BY CHARLOTTE MASON

Pages 34 to 40

What is an Idea?—A live thing of the mind, according to the older philosophers, from Plato to Bacon, from Bacon to Coleridge We say of an idea that it strikes us, impresses us, seizes us, takes possession of us, rules us; and our common speech is, as usual, truer to fact than the conscious thought which it expresses.

We do not in the least exaggerate in ascribing this sort of action and power to an idea. We form an ideal—a, so to speak, embodied idea—and our ideal exercises the very strongest formative influence upon us. Why do you devote yourself to this pursuit, that cause? 'Because twenty years ago such and such an idea struck me,' is the sort of history which might be given of every purposeful life—every life devoted to the working out of an idea

Now is it not marvellous that, recognising as we do the potency of ideas, both the word and the conception it covers enter so little into our thought of education? Coleridge brings the conception of an 'idea' within the sphere of the scientific thought of today; not as that thought is expressed in Psychology—a term which he himself launched upon the world with an apology for it as an *insolens verbum*, but in that science of the correlation and interaction of mind and brain, which is at present rather clumsily expressed in such terms as 'mental physiology' and 'psycho-physiology.'

In his Method Coleridge gives us the following illustration of the rise and progress of an idea:—

Rise and Progress of an Idea—"We can recall no incident of human history that impresses the imagination more deeply than the moment when Columbus, on an unknown ocean, first perceived that startling fact, the change of the magnetic needle.

How many such instances occur in history when the ideas of Nature (presented to chosen minds by a Higher Power than Nature herself) suddenly unfold, as it were, in prophetic succession, systematic views destined to produce the most important revolutions in the state of man.

The clear spirit of Columbus was doubtless eminently methodical. He saw distinctly that great leading idea which authorised the poor pilot to become a 'promiser of kingdoms.'"

Genesis of an Idea—Notice the genesis of such ideas—'presented to chosen minds by a Higher Power than Nature'; notice how accurately this history of an idea fits in with what we know of the history of great inventions and discoveries, with that of the ideas which rule our own lives; and how well does it correspond with that key to the origin of 'practical' ideas which we find elsewhere:—

"Doth the ploughman plough continually to.... open and break the clods of his ground? When he hath made plain the face thereof, doth he not cast abroad' the fitches, and scatter the cumin, and put in the wheat in rows, and the barley in the appointed place, and the spelt in the border thereof? For his God doth instruct him aright, and doth teach him.... "Bread corn is ground; for he will not ever be threshing it . . This also cometh forth from the Lord of hosts, which is wonderful in counsel and excellent in wisdom."

An Idea may exist as an 'Appetency.'—Ideas may invest as an atmosphere, rather than strike as a weapon. 'The idea may exist in a clear, distinct, definite form, as that of a circle in the mind of a geometrician; or it may be a mere instinct, a vague appetency towards something,... like the impulse which fills the young poet's eyes with tears, he knows not why: To excite this 'appetency towards something'—towards things lovely, honest, and or good report, is the earliest and most important ministry of the educator.

How shall these indefinite ideas which manifest themselves in appetency be imparted? They are not to be given of set purpose, nor taken at set times—They are held in that thought—environment which surrounds the child as an atmosphere, which he breathes as his breath of life; and this atmosphere in which the child inspires his unconscious ideas of right living emanates from his parents.

Every look of gentleness and tone of reverence, every word of kindness and act of help, passes into the thought-environment, the very atmosphere which the child breathes; he does not think of these things, may never think of them, but all his life long they excite that 'vague appetency towards something' out of which most of his actions spring. Oh, wonderful and dreadful presence of the little child in the midst!

A Child draws Inspiration from the Casual Life around him—That he should take direction and inspiration from all the casual life about him, should make our poor words and ways the starting-point from which, and in the direction of which, he develops—this is a thought which makes the best of us hold our breath.

There is no way of escape for parents; they must needs be as 'inspirers' to their children, because about them hangs, as its atmosphere about a planet the thought-environment of the child, from which he derives those enduring ideas which express themselves as a life-long 'appetency' towards things sordid or things lovely, things earthly or divine.

Order and Progress of Definite Ideas—Let us now hear Coleridge on the subject of those definite ideas which are not inhaled as air; but conveyed as meat to the mind:

"From the first, or initiative idea, as from a seed, successive ideas germinate."

"Events and images, the lively and spirit-stirring machinery of the external world, are like light and air and moisture to the seed of the mind, which would else rot and perish"

"The paths in which we may pursue a methodical course are manifold, and at the head of each stands its peculiar and guiding idea."

"Those ideas are as regularly subordinate in dignity as the paths to which they point are various and eccentric in direction. The world has suffered much, in modern times, from a subversion of the natural and necessary order of Science.... from summoning reason and faith to the bar of that limited physical experience to which, by the true laws or method, they owe no obedience."

"Progress follows the path of the idea from which it sets out; requiring, however, a constant wakefulness of mind to keep it within the due limits of its course. Hence the orbits of thought, so to speak, must differ among themselves as the initiative ideas differ."

Platonic Doctrine of Ideas—Have we not here the corollary to, and the explanation of that law of unconscious cerebration which results in our 'ways of thinking: which shapes our character, rules our destiny?

Thoughtful minds consider that the new light which biology is throwing upon the laws of mind is bringing to the front once more the Platonic doctrine, that "An idea is a distinguishable power, self-affirmed, and seen in its unity with the Eternal Essence."

Ideas alone matter in Education—The whole subject is profound, but as practical as it is profound. We must disabuse our minds of the theory that the functions of education are, in the main, gymnastic.

In the early years of the child's life it makes, perhaps, little apparent difference whether his parents start with the notion that to educate is to fill a receptacle, inscribe a tablet, mould plastic matter, or nourish a life; but in the end we shall find that only those ideas which have fed his life are taken into the being of the child; all the rest is thrown away, or worse, is like sawdust in the system, an impediment and an injury to the vital processes—

How the Educational Formula should run—This is, perhaps, how the educational formula should run: Education is a life; that life is sustained on ideas; ideas are of spiritual origin; and, 'God has made us so' that we get them chiefly as we convey them to one another.

The duty of parents is to sustain a child's Inner life with ideas as they sustain his body with food. The child is an eclectic; he may choose this or that; therefore, in the morning sow thy seed, and in the evening withhold not thy hand, for thou knowest not which shall prosper, whether this or that, or whether they both shall be alike good.

The child has affinities with evil as well as with good; therefore, hedge him about from any chance lodgement of evil ideas.

The initial idea begets subsequent ideas; therefore, take care that children get right primary ideas on the great relations and duties of life.

Every study, every line of thought, has its 'guiding idea'; therefore, the study of a child makes for living education in proportion as it is quickened by the guiding idea 'which stands at the head.'

***'Infallible Reason'; what is it?**—In a word, our much boasted 'infallible reason'—is it not the involuntary thought which follows the initial idea upon necessary logical lines? Given, the starting idea, and the conclusion may be predicated almost to a certainty. We get into the way of thinking such and such manner of thoughts, and of coming to such and such conclusions, ever further and further removed from the starting-point, but on the same lines.*

There is structural adaptation in the brain tissue to the manner of thoughts we think—a place and a way for them to run in. Thus we see how the destiny of a life is shaped in the nursery, by the reverent naming of the Divine Name; by the light scoff at holy things; by the thought of duty the little child gets who is made to finish conscientiously his little task; by the hardness of heart that comes to the child who hears the faults or sorrows of others spoken of lightly.

CHAPTER 4.
LIVING BOOKS

Now that you have had two opportunities to read Charlotte Mason's own work I hope you are feeling good about it and enjoying what you are reading and learning. One special thing is that you are reading Charlotte Mason's work, rather than just reading what someone else has said about her work. It gives a good feeling of satisfaction, doesn't it?

If you can keep up with your reading, and resist the temptation to put it off or skip those pages, you will be glad in the end. By reading along with me each chapter you are guaranteeing that you will read enough of Charlotte Mason's work to have a reasonable understanding of what she wanted to teach. And you will be getting the maximum benefit from this book.

So far, you have learned how to plan a timetable, and how to fit all your chosen subjects into your week. And you have a good understanding of the power of ideas in influencing a person's life. Now, let's look in more detail at a practical aspect of homeschooling. Let's talk about something which is close to the heart of every homeschooler I have met – books!

LIVING BOOKS

Someone once joked that when she first heard the term 'living books' she wasn't sure whether she was supposed to feed a living book or read it.

The term, LIVING BOOKS originated with Charlotte Mason to describe a book which contains ideas.

But if some books are living books, does that mean that some books are ... not living books? That's right. Some books are not worth reading, and some of those books are very prominent in homeschool circles too.

Let's take some time now to look more closely at the qualities of a living book, so that we will be able to recognise a living book when we see one.

WHAT IS A LIVING BOOK?

In Volume 3, page 177 Charlotte Mason said: *Ideas come to us from the mind of the thinker.* So we can know that a living book must put us in touch with the mind of the author.

- In Volume 2, page 231, Charlotte Mason says of living books: *… we know that there is a storehouse of thought wherein we may find all the great ideas that have moved the world. We are above all things anxious to give the child the key to this storehouse.* So we can know that a living book is a storehouse of ideas.
- In Volume 3, page 178, Charlotte Mason says, the child must enjoy the book and it must make an impact on his mind. So we can know that a living book must convey knowledge.
- In Volume 6, page 7, Charlotte Mason says: *The books used are, whenever possible, literary in style.* So we can know that a living book might convey facts in a story form, but it is not limited to stories. However, it will always be well written.

WHY ARE LIVING BOOKS IMPORTANT?

I think it's important to work out what a living book is, and to become very discerning in our choice of books. It's important for us, but it's crucial for our children. The thing is, whatever we receive when we are children we accept as being normal and right.

For example, if our children are given poor quality books they will accept the books as fine and good. When they grow up they will have fond memories of those poor quality books without any discernment about the quality.

On the other hand, if we give our children worthy books of quality they will also grow up with a fondness for that type of book.

And what difference does it make? Why worry about the quality? Does it matter? I think it does. If we give our children the best then we give them a taste for beauty and rich quality.

If we introduce them to great minds through the writings of great writers we enlarge the world of our children more than any amount of time spent watching the Discovery channel on television. We stretch their minds. We enrich their spirits and fill their minds with all that is laudable and worthy.

Most of us learn moral values from stories. By providing our young people with well written stories of heroes, we offer role models who will inspire them to aim high better than any 'values clarification' lessons or 'critical thinking' lessons.

Through the best books we can offer our children the opportunity to live a rich, full life in all its aspects.

QUESTIONS TO CONSIDER

Here are some questions to prompt some thought, and maybe some discussion with your Significant Other

- List the qualities of a living book.
- Try and list a couple of living books.
- Why should children use living books?

Charlotte Mason wrote: *My plea is, ...that they shall be introduced to no subject whatever through compendiums, abstracts, or selections; that the young—shall learn what history is, what literature is, what life is, from the living books of those who know. I know it can be done, because it is being done on a considerable scale.* (Volume 3, page 247)

- What do you think of this?

Charlotte Mason wrote: *It is not important that many books should be read; but it is important that only good books should be read; and read with such ease and pleasant leisure, that they become to the hearers so much mental property for life.* (Volume 5, page 223).

- Do you agree with her? Why? Do you see any benefit from reading a few good books?
- What is wrong with reading books which might not be considered worthy or 'living'?

SUMMARY

In this chapter:

- I have talked about 'Living Books', what they are, how to recognise them and how to use them.
- I have asked some questions to help you explore the idea of living books.

- If you have spent time answering the questions then you will have done some deep thinking, and you will be better equipped to identify the best books and choose the best books for your children.

ASSIGNMENT

- Spend some time completing the questions in the chapters. Give your answers some thought. It will pay off later.
- Look on your bookshelves and see if you can find some living books. Books that you are sure are living books. Be confident in your opinion.
- Read what Charlotte Mason says about living books. The quotations are:
- Volume 2, page 279
- Volume 3, page 124, page 177, page 178, page 214, pages 226, 227
- Volume 6, page 12 and page 303

SUPPLEMENT

LIVING BOOKS

Quotations from Charlotte Mason

Volume 2, page 231

We trust much to Good Books.——Once more, we know that there is a storehouse of thought wherein we may find all the great ideas that have moved the world. We are above all things anxious to give the child the key to this storehouse. The education of the day, it is said, does not produce reading people.

We are determined that the children shall love books, therefore we do not interpose ourselves between the book and the child. We read him his Tanglewood Tales, and when he is a little older his Plutarch, not trying to break up or water down, but leaving the child's mind to deal with the matter as it can.

Volume 2, page 279

Children must have the Best Books—One more thing is of vital importance; children must have books, living books; the best are not too good for them; anything less than the best is not good enough; and if it is needful to exercise economy, let go everything that belongs to soft and luxurious living before letting go the duty of supplying the books, and the frequent changes of books, which are necessary for the constant stimulation of the child's intellectual life.

We need not say one word about the necessity for living thought in the teacher; it is only so far as he is intellectually alive that he can be effective in the wonderful process which we glibly call 'education.'

Volume 3, page 124

I should like to say here that a sort of unconscious, inherited parsimony, coming down to us from the days when incomes were smaller and books were fewer, sometimes causes parents to restrict their children unduly in the matter of lesson-books—living books, varied from time to time, and not thumbed over from one schoolroom generation to another until the very sight of them is a weariness to the flesh. But the subject of the intellectual sustenance of children upon ideas is so.

Volume 3, page 177

In their power of giving impulse and stirring emotion is another use of books, the right books; but that is just the question -which are the right books? ..The 'hundred best books for the schoolroom' may be put down on a list, but not by me.

I venture to propose one or two principles in the matter of school-books, and shall leave the far more difficult part, the application of those principles, to the reader. For example, I think we owe it to children to let them dig their knowledge, of whatever subject, for themselves out of the fit book; and this for two reasons:

What a child digs for is his own possession;

What is poured into his ear, like the idle song of a pleasant singer, floats out as lightly as it came in, and is rarely assimilated.

...

Again, as I have already said, ideas must reach us directly from the mind of the thinker, and it is chiefly by means of the books they have written that we get into touch with the best minds.

Volume 3, page 178

So much for the right books; the right use of them is another matter. The children must enjoy the book, The ideas it holds must each make that sudden, delightful impact upon their minds, must cause that intellectual stir, which mark the inception of an idea.

Volume 3, page 214

Every scholar of six years old and upwards should study with 'delight' his own, living, books on every subject in a pretty wide curriculum. Children between six and eight must for the most part have their books read to them.

Volume 3, pp 226—227

Children must be Educated on Books .*-A corollary of the principle that education is the science of relations, is, that no education seems to be worth the name which has not made children at home in the world of books, and so related them, mind to mind, with thinkers who have dealt with knowledge.*

We reject epitomes, compilations, and their like, and put into children's hands books which, long or short, are living. Thus it becomes a large part of the teacher's work to help children to deal with their books; so that the oral lesson and lecture are but small matters in education, and are used chiefly to summarise or to expand or illustrate.

Too much faith is commonly placed in oral lessons and lectures; "to be poured into like a bucket," as says Carlyle, "is not exhilarating to any soul"; neither is it exhilarating to have every difficulty explained to weariness, or to have the explanation teased out of one by questions. "I will not be put to the question. Don't you consider, sir, that these are not the manners of a gentleman? I will not be baited with what and why; what is this? what is that? why is a cow's tail long? why is a fox's tail bushy?" said Dr Johnson. This is what children think, though they say nothing.

Oral lessons have their occasional use, and when they are fitly given it is the children who ask the questions. Perhaps it is not wholesome or quite honest for a teacher to pose as a source of all knowledge and to give 'lovely' lessons. Such lessons are titillating for the moment, but they give children the minimum of mental labour, and the result is much the same as that left on older persons by the reading of a magazine.

We find, on the other hand, that in working through a considerable book, which may take two or three years to master, the interest of boys and girls is well sustained to the end; they develop an intelligent curiosity as to causes and consequences, and are in fact educating themselves.

Volume 6, page 12

We owe it to every child to put him in communication with great minds that he may get at great thought; with the minds that is of those who have left us great works; and the only vital method of education appears to be that children should read worthy books.

Volume 6, page 303

'What is knowledge?' the reader asks. We can give only a negative answer. Knowledge is not instruction, information, scholarship, a well-stored memory. It is passed, like the light of a torch, from mind to mind, and the flame can be kindled at original minds only.

Thought, we know, breeds thought; it is as vital thought

touches our minds that our ideas are vitalised, and out of our ideas comes our conduct of life,

The direct and immediate impact of great minds upon his own mind is necessary to the education of a child... Most of us can get into touch with original minds chiefly through books ..."

CHAPTER 5.
DOWN WITH TWADDLE!

By now, you have probably started noticing a change in some of your thoughts about education. You will also start to be more aware of certain aspects of your child's learning and the way you relate to him. This can be very challenging to begin with and then it will become freeing.

Let's take things up a notch and consider in more detail how to recognise a living book, and how to recognise twaddle.

But first, I have some good news and some bad news for you. Do you want the good news or the bad news first?

Yep! Thought so! You want the bad news first, don't you? You want to get the bad news over and done with quickly, and that's a good idea. Because the good news is really good news.

So here's the bad news, first. If I could tell you only one thing about choosing books for your child, it would be this. There isn't a list of age-appropriate books for you to give to your child. You will find lots of lists, all over the place. You will see some books on many different lists. You will even see books with lists of books for your children to read.

But, there is not a list of books for you to work through which will guarantee a good education with no 'holes'. In fact, Charlotte Mason said this herself:

The 'hundred best books for the schoolroom' may be put down on a list, but not by me. I venture to propose one or two principles in the matter of school-books, and shall leave the far more difficult part, the application of those principles, to the reader. (Volume 3, page 177)

And now, here is the good news. There are more good books for you to choose from for your child, no matter what the subject or what age your child, than you can shake a stick at. And although I can't give you a list, I can teach you how to make your own list. You can download some of my book lists from http://charlottemasonmadeeasy.com/bookbonus

HOW TO MAKE YOUR OWN LIST OF LIVING BOOKS

What did Charlotte Mason have to say about books? She wanted only worthy books for her students to learn from, she talked about having only the very best for the children:

...we owe it to every child to put him in communication with great minds that he may get at great thoughts; with the minds, that is, of those who have left us great works; and the only vital method of education appears to be that children should read worthy books, many worthy books.

So we need to put our children in touch with the great minds and then step back and allow the great minds to speak directly to our children without interference from us.

I have made a list of nine questions that you can ask when making your tailor-made list of living books for your family.

NINE QUESTIONS TO ASK TO DETERMINE IF A BOOK IS "LIVING"

1. Is this a book that I want to read myself, or is it one that I think would be 'good' for my child to read? This is probably the simplest and most important rule in your choosing. For example, I absolutely love historical novels by Cynthia Harnett and Rosemary Sutcliff, so I am going to choose and recommend those to my children. I also really enjoy Jean-Henri Fabre's science books, so they are on the list too. And so it goes on.

2. Is this the best book I can find on the subject I am teaching? This is really helpful to you when you are choosing books, because you are narrowing down the field and it's easier to see what you want. It's like going into a dress shop to look for a purple dress. You ignore all the other colours. The purple dresses call out to you to come and choose them.

3. Is this book written by people who absolutely love their subject? When someone loves what they do they write with passion and they communicate that love and passion to the reader. Just think about the last really good book you read...

4. Is this a text book? Only use curriculum books and text books as a last resort. Curriculum books and

text books are written for classroom teachers who need to cover an artificial curriculum. They are usually written by a group of people and they have to fit in with a long list of requirements. You are not restricted by school boards or education ministers. You can choose a book on a subject to suit your particular type and age of child. So your child will get a custom-chosen book on a subject written by someone who loves their subject.

5. Is this book beautiful? Books appeal to me on many levels. I like the smell, size, and feel of a book, and these things will influence my decision to buy. In fact, I've become quite fussy over the years, so now I would choose hardback over paperback. I would not buy a second hand book which smells bad or has a lot of foxing (the brown spots you see around the edges of the pages) or is tatty and worn, unless it was a very special book. When I have nice copies of books I want to pick the books up, and I take immense pleasure in reading a nice copy.

6. Is this a book that I already read and love? Books that you have already read and love are the best, and they should be at the top of your list. This is a no-brainer, isn't it? If you love the book then you will talk about it with affection and your child is likely to be more interested in reading it himself.

7. Is this a book that someone would want to read anyway, and not just because they are studying it as a 'school subject'? When you are choosing books to use in educating your children, go for real books that anybody would want to read.

8. Has this book been recommended to you by someone you trust? Look first at recommendations from people you trust; that's a great place to start.

9. Does this book inspire, encourage, challenge, teach, enrich, and edify in some way? Choose books which are well written. Avoid books which are sloppily written, use clichés, have an 'agenda' and patronise the reader.

WHAT IS TWADDLE?

Twaddle (rhymes with 'waddle') is a commonly used English word referring to poor quality, trivial talk. It is diluted information served to children in an attempt to help them understand something. It's talking down to children. It's treating children disrespectfully in terms of understanding what the child can assimilate. It's baby-talk. Charlotte Mason talks about 'diluted knowledge'. Can you get the idea of what that might be? Here's what Charlotte Mason says about diluted knowledge and twaddle:

Volume 1, page 175

Diluted Knowledge.—But, poor children, they are too often badly used by their best friends in the matter of the knowledge offered them. Grown-up people who are not mothers talk and think far more childishly than the child does in their efforts to approach his mind. If a child talk twaddle, it is because his elders are in the habit of talking twaddle to him; leave him to himself, and his remarks are wise and sensible so far as his small experience guides him. Mothers seldom talk down to their children; they are too intimate with the little people, and have, therefore, too much respect for them: but professional teachers, whether the writers of books or the givers of lessons are too apt to present a single grain of pure knowledge in a whole gallon of talk, imposing upon the child the labour of discerning the grain and of extracting it from the worthless flood.

Charlotte Mason believed that teachers shouldn't interfere with a child's acquiring knowledge and information from a 'great mind'. And when teachers do interfere, they usually produce twaddle. Do you recognise this scenario?

Volume 1, page 188

Teachers mediate too much.*—There are still, probably, Kindergartens where a great deal of twaddle is talked in song and story, where the teacher conceives that to make poems for the children herself and to compose tunes for their singing and to draw pictures for their admiration, is to fulfil her function to the uttermost. The children might echo Wordsworth's complaint of 'the world,' and say, the teacher is too much with us, late and soon. Everything is directed, expected, suggested. No other personality out of book, picture, or song, no, not even that of*

Nature herself, can get at the children without the mediation of the teacher. No room is left for spontaneity or personal initiation on their part.

Charlotte Mason believed that there was never an excuse for twaddle, no matter what subject or how old or young the child is. She believed that young children can cope with big concepts. And if you have read my short biography on Charlotte Mason then you might remember how Charlotte Mason had a clear memory of her own mother telling her the name of the book she was reading which was "Pope's Homer's Odyssey"

Volume 1, page 205

Even for their earliest reading lessons, it is unnecessary to put twaddle into the hands of children.

Volume 1, page 226

…when there is so much noble poetry within a child's compass, the pity of it that he should be allowed to learn twaddle!

Volume 1, page 229

*…**Lesson-Books**—A child has not begun his education until he has acquired the habit of reading to himself, with interest and pleasure, books fully on a level with his intelligence. I am speaking now of his lesson-books, which are all too apt to be written in a style of insufferable twaddle, probably because they are written by persons who have never chanced to meet a child. All who know children know that they do not talk twaddle and do not like it, and prefer that which appeals to their understanding. Their lesson-books should offer matter for their reading, whether aloud or to themselves; therefore they should be written with literary power. As for the matter of these books, let us remember that children can take in ideas and principles, whether the latter be moral or mechanical, as quickly and clearly as we do ourselves (perhaps more so); but detailed processes, lists and summaries, blunt the edge of a child's delicate mind. Therefore, the selection of their first lesson-books is a matter of grave importance, because it rests with these to give children the idea that knowledge is supremely attractive and that reading is delightful. Once the habit of reading his lesson-book with delight is set up in a child, his education is—not completed, but—*

ensured; he will go on for himself in spite of the obstructions which school too commonly throws in his way.

SUMMARY

In this chapter:

- I've given you a list of questions to guide you, and to teach you how to recognise a living book.
- I've explained why you need to make your own list of living books and I've given you a list of nine questions to ask yourself as you make your choices and build your list and your library. And I've told you about twaddle – what it is and why you shouldn't use it.

ASSIGNMENT

- Use your checklist to go through your book shelves and see how many of your books are living books; worthy books that you want to read and use to teach your children. Be confident in your choices; Charlotte Mason isn't going to come to your house and disagree with your choices, and neither am I.
- Now this might be hard for you: collect the books that you KNOW are not worthy and put them in a box to give away or throw away. When you've done that, remember to congratulate yourself. You have space on your shelves now for truly worthy books!
- Read: Volume 3, pages 177 – 180 and Volume 3, pages 228 – 330

SUPPLEMENT

Quotations from The Original Homeschool Series by Charlotte Mason

VOLUME 3, PAGES 177 – 180

Principles on which to select School-books.—*In their power of giving impulse and stirring emotion is another use of books, the right books; but that is just the question—which are the right books?—a point upon which I should not wish to play Sir Oracle.*

The 'hundred best books for the schoolroom' may be put down on a list, but not by me. I venture to propose one or two principles in the matter of school-books, and shall leave the far more difficult part, the application of those principles, to the reader.

For example, I think we owe it to children to let them dig their knowledge, of whatever subject, for themselves out of the fit book; and this for two reasons:

- *What a child digs for is his own possession;*
- *What is poured into his ear, like the idle song of a pleasant singer, floats out as lightly as it came in, and is rarely assimilated.*

I do not mean to say that the lecture and the oral lesson are without their uses; but these uses are, to give impulse and to order knowledge; and not to convey knowledge, or to afford us that part of our education which comes of fit knowledge, fitly given.

Again, as I have already said, ideas must reach us directly from the mind of the thinker, and it is chiefly by means of the books they have written that we get into touch with the best minds.

Marks of a Fit Book.—*As to the distinguishing marks of a book for the school-room, a word or two may be said. A fit book is not necessarily a big book. John Quincy Adams, aged nine, wrote to his father for the fourth volume of Smollett for his private reading, though, as he owned up, his thoughts were running on birds' eggs; and perhaps some of us remember going religiously through the many volumes of Alison's History of Europe with a private feeling that the bigness of the book swelled the virtue of the reader.*

But now, big men write little books, to be used with discretion; because sometimes the little books are no more than abstracts, the dry bones of the subjects; and sometimes the little books are fresh and living.

Again, we need not always insist that a book should be written by the original thinker. It sometimes happens that second-rate minds have assimilated the matter in hand, and are able to give out what is their own thought (only because they have made it their own) in a form more suitable for our purpose than that of the first-hand thinkers.

We cannot make any hard and fast rule—a big book or a little book, a book at first-hand or at second-hand; either may be right provided we have it in us to discern a living book, quick, and informed with the ideas proper to the subject of which it treats.

How to use the Right Books.—So much for the right books; the right use of them is another matter. The children must enjoy the book. The ideas it holds must each make that sudden, delightful impact upon their minds, must cause that intellectual stir, which mark the inception of an idea.

The teacher's part in this regard is to see and feel for himself, and then to rouse his pupils by an appreciative look or word; but to beware how he deadens the impression by a flood of talk. Intellectual sympathy is very stimulating; but we have all been in the case of the little girl who said, "Mother, I think I could understand if you did not explain quite so much."

A teacher said of her pupil, "I find it so hard to tell whether she has really grasped a thing or whether she has only got the mechanical hang of it." Children are imitative monkeys, and it is the 'mechanical hang' that is apt to arrive after a deluge of explanation.

Children must Labour.—This, of getting ideas out of them, is by no means all we must do with books. 'In all labour there is profit,' at any rate in some labour; and the labour of thought is what his book must induce in the child. He must generalise, classify, infer, judge, visualise, discriminate, labour in one way or another, with that capable mind of his, until the substance of his book is assimilated or rejected, according as he shall determine; for the determination rests with him and not with his teacher.

Value of Narration.—The simplest way of dealing with

a paragraph or a chapter is to require the child to narrate its contents after a single attentive reading,—one reading, however slow, should be made a condition; for we are all too apt to make sure we shall have another opportunity of finding out 'what 'tis all about' There is the chapterly review if we fail to get a clear grasp of the news of the day; and, if we fail a second time, there is a monthly or a quarterly review or an annual summing up: in fact, many of us let present-day history pass by us with easy minds, feeling sure that, in the end, we shall be compelled to see the bearings of events.

This is a bad habit to get into; and we should do well to save our children by not giving them the vague expectation of second and third and tenth opportunities to do that which should have been done at first.

A Single Careful Reading.—There is much difference between intelligent reading, which the pupil should do in silence, and a mere parrot-like cramming up of contents; and it is not a bad test of education to be able to give the points of a description, the sequence of a series of incidents, the links in a chain of argument, correctly, after a single careful reading.

This is a power which a barrister, a publisher, a scholar, labours to acquire; and it is a power which children can acquire with great ease, and once acquired, the gulf is bridged which divides the reading from the non-reading community.

Other Ways of using Books.—But this is only one way to use books: others are to enumerate the statements in a given paragraph or chapter; to analyse a chapter, to divide it into paragraphs under proper headings, to tabulate and classify series; to trace cause to consequence and consequence to cause; to discern character and perceive how character and circumstance interact; to get lessons of life and conduct, or the living knowledge which makes for science, out of books; all this is possible for school boys and girls, and until they have begun to use books for themselves in such ways, they can hardly be said to have begun their education.

The Teacher's Part.—The teacher's part is, in the first place, to see what is to be done, to look over the of the day in advance and see what mental discipline, as well as what vital knowledge, this and that lesson afford; and then to set such questions and such tasks as shall give full scope to his pupils' mental activity.

Let marginal notes be freely made, as neatly and beautifully as may be, for books should be handled with reverence. Let numbers, letters, underlining be used to help the eye and to save the needless fag of writing abstracts.

Let the pupil write for himself half a dozen questions which cover the passage studied; he need not write the answers if he be taught that the mind can know nothing but what it can produce in the form of an answer to a question put by the mind to itself.

Disciplinary Devices must not come between Children and the Soul of the Book.—These few hints by no means cover the disciplinary uses of a good school-book; but let us be careful that our disciplinary devices, and our mechanical devices to secure and tabulate the substance of knowledge, do not come between the children and that which is the soul of the book, the living thought it contains. Science is doing so much for us in these days, nature is drawing so close to us, art is unfolding so much meaning to us, the world is becoming so rich for us, that we are a little in danger of neglecting the art of deriving sustenance from books.

Let us not in such wise impoverish our lives and the lives of our children; for, to quote the golden words of Milton: "Books are not absolutely dead things, but do contain a potency of life in them to be as active as that soul was, whose progeny they are; nay, they do preserve, as in a vial, the purest efficacy 'and extraction of that living intellect that bred them. As good almost kill a man, as kill a good book; who kills a man kills a good reasonable creature, God's image; but he who destroys a good book, kills reason itself-kills the image of God, as it were, in the eye."

Volume 3, pages 228 – 330

SCHOOL-BOOKS

Books that supply the Sustenance of Ideas.—Mr. H. G. Wells has put his finger on the place when he says that the selection of the right schoolbooks is a great function of the educator. I am not at all sure that his remedy is the right one—or that a body of experts and a hundred thousand pounds would, in truth, provide the manner of schoolbooks that reach children. They are kittle cattle, and, though they will plod on obediently over any of the hundreds of dry-as-dust volumes issued by the publishers under the heading of 'School Books,' or of 'Education,' they keep all such books in the outer court, and allow them no access to their minds.

A book may be long or short, old or new, easy or hard, written by a great man or a lesser man, and yet be the living book which finds its way to the mind of a young reader. The expert is not the person to choose; the children themselves are the experts in this case. A single page will elicit a verdict; but the unhappy thing is, this verdict is not betrayed; it is acted upon in the opening or closing of the door of the mind.

Many excellent and admirable school-books appreciated by masters are on the Index Expurgatorius of the school-boy; and that is why he takes nothing in and gives nothing out. The master must have it in him to distinguish between twaddle and simplicity, and between vivacity and life.

For the rest, he must experiment or test the experiments of others, being assured of one thing—that a book serves the ends of education only as it is vital. But this subject has been treated at some length in an earlier chapter.

Books and Oral Teaching.—Having found the right book, let the master give the book the lead and be content himself with a second place. The lecture must be subordinated to the book. The business of the teacher is to put his class in the right attitude towards their book by a word or two of his own interest in the matter contained, of his own delight in the manner of the author. But boys get knowledge only as they dig for it. Labour prepares the way for assimilation, that mental process which converts information into knowledge; and the effort of taking in the sequence of thought of his author is worth to the boy a great deal of oral teaching.

Do teachers always realise the paralysing and stupefying effect that a flood of talk has upon the mind? The inspired talk of an orator no doubt wakens a response and is listened to with tense attention; but few of us claim to be inspired, and we are sometimes aware of the difficulty of holding the attention of a class.

We blame ourselves, whereas the blame lies in the instrument we employ—the more or less diluted oral lesson or lecture, in place of the living and arresting book. We cannot do without the oral lesson—to introduce, to illustrate, to amplify, to sum up.

My stipulation is that oral lessons should be few and far between, and that the child who has to walk through life,—and has to find his intellectual life in books or go without,—shall not be first taught to go upon crutches.

CHAPTER 6.
NARRATION

This is always a popular subject as we discuss the famous 'Charlotte Mason' teaching skill of narration, which at first looks easy, but many people find hard. In actual fact, there are some secrets to teaching narration and I would like to share them with you here.

One of the first things people learn when they start hearing about Charlotte Mason's philosophy of education is that Charlotte Mason advocated "narration".

WHAT IS 'NARRATION'?

It's simply telling back what the child has just heard or read.

The way it goes is that you read a passage to your child once and then he tells you in his own words what the passage said.

This sounds too simple at first, but if you try narrating yourself you'll see that it's quite a learned art.

Think about it:

- Have you tried giving someone directions to a shop or a park or someone else's house when you have been only once?
- Have you tried to tell someone the plot of a story you are reading?
- Have you tried to tell someone about a movie or television programme you have watched?
- Can you do any of the above without missing out anything important and without getting in a muddle about it?

It's not always easy to remember everything in the right order and sometimes you can miss out quite important parts of the story by mistake, can't you? Sometimes, I can't even remember the names of the main characters in a story, so that I find myself referring to them as 'the guy' or 'the girl' or 'the guy's friend'. Does that sound familiar?

THE BENEFIT OF NARRATION

Something happens in the brain when you start to tell back or repeat what you have just learned. You have to order things in your mind; you have to sort and file the thoughts and ideas. You have to 'own' the thoughts and ideas. You internalise the ideas. You are engaged, and you have to think!

We have all heard the old comment, 'if you want to learn something then teach it', haven't we? Well it makes sense, doesn't it?

You might like to consider narration as a type of storytelling.

STARTING NARRATION

When you first start narration with your child it's good to remember to go slowly, and to set realistic expectations. But how slow is slow? And what is it realistic to expect from a child?

Well, first, it helps to know that narration is a skill to be learned. Your child might not find it easy to begin with. And it's also likely that you will meet with resistance from your child. But don't worry if you do; I will be giving you a few tips to help you with that.

WHEN TO START NARRATION WITH YOUR CHILD

Watch out for narrations taking place naturally. For example, your child might describe a game she has been playing. Or she might be very excited about an event that happened at a relative's house, and she wants to tell you all about it. Or she wants to describe a movie, programme or book that she really enjoyed.

When this happens, LET HER FLY! But be careful that you don't push it. You don't want her to clam up and refuse to tell you things in case you turn it into a 'narration'.

These spontaneous narrations will start developing as soon as your child can speak in intelligible sentences. You can look out for narrations of events all through toddlerhood and preschool. For example, your child might come home from the zoo and describe some of the events to Dad or Grandma; that's narration. And by the time your child is rising six you will be asking for narrations on subjects of your choice.

HOW TO START NARRATION

Start with a very short piece for oral narration. Charlotte Mason said that Aesop's Fables are great for beginners. And I think that's still a great choice. It will work well for children of five or six or so. And it's a quick way to start with an older child.

If you are teaching narration to an older child, you can start with Aesop's Fables to get the idea, and then you can move on to paragraphs and a page or two of an age-appropriate book.

When you start with Aesop's Fables, you can read aloud one of the fables and then ask your child to tell you the story back. I always found that my child liked to try and guess the moral of the story too.

You can find various copies of Aesop's Fables in the library or in many book shops.

NINE HELPFUL HINTS FOR TEACHING NARRATION

1. Before you start reading, warn your child that you will ask him to tell you what you have read.
2. Make a note of anything unusual before you start reading. For example, any unusual names, or any dates. And write these on a blackboard/ whiteboard or on paper, where your child can see them. This helps to set the scene for your child.
3. Don't read for longer than a few minutes before asking for a narration. This means that a whole story or a whole chapter will be too much to begin with. Start with a couple of paragraphs or a page or two. You will gradually build up to a chapter or a whole story.
4. Just ask your child to tell you about what you have read to him.
5. Whatever your child says to you is enough and is fine. (I'll tell you why later.)
6. Don't prompt him or remind him of things.
7. Don't allow your child to keep interrupting the story with questions while you are reading. Encourage your child to wait and listen, and see if his question gets answered.

8. It helps the 'interrupter' if you read extra slowly. Especially if the language style is unfamiliar or difficult.
9. Narration is ideally suited to teaching more than one child because each child will listen carefully in case they get asked for a narration, although you may only ask one child.

WHAT ABOUT WRITTEN NARRATIONS?

Written narrations won't start until the child is about ten, and then it is a very gradual transition from oral to written narrations.

What you are really aiming for here, is that the child will read a piece just once, but he will read it very attentively, and carefully. Then he will write about what he has read.

Narration is so different from the more usual exercise where the child might 'research' an article on the Internet and then tweak and spin it so that the words are slightly different, and the article looks original when it isn't. The child's brain really hasn't done very much work to produce this sort of writing, and the child hasn't really learnt or internalised anything on the topic.

Narration is real learning. Learning with full attention and engagement and involvement.

BUILDING UP "NARRATION STAMINA"

Narration gets easier over time. Honestly. It WILL get easier. I know it can feel boring and hard and children sometimes rebel and say they don't like it. But don't be discouraged, narration will get easier and it does pay off in terms of teaching a child to think.

At first, he will probably miss important bits out, or tell things out of order. All that is okay and it's better not to correct him. The reason for that is that his narration actually tells you what your child knows and how much he understood of the lesson or piece read.

From this you can know what your child needs to know, and you can plan accordingly.

But then you will gradually start to see improvement in his narrations and you know that something is clicking and something is working!

FOR MORE EXPERIENCED NARRATORS

As your child becomes more experienced in narrating she will improve in ability and in quality of narrations. She will also gain confidence and it will get easier for her. And for you too.

Narration doesn't only consist of a child telling back a story in her own words. It can be a drawing or a painting. In fact, it can even be a game; have you ever had the intense pleasure of overhearing your child playing a game and incorporating something that you have taught her?

For example, maybe he is playing a character in history, and starts to speak in the same style of a book you have been reading him about Robin Hood. It feels really good, doesn't it?

IF YOU ARE FINDING NARRATION HARD

If you are finding narration hard, you might like to try different ways of framing your request for narrations. For example, you could ask:

- Tell me all you remember about the passage
- Tell me about this in your own words.

You could use words like:
- Tell me...
- Explain how...
- Describe ...
- Why did ...
- What did you learn about ...
- Draw a picture of ...

And when you find that narration is hard, remember:
- Narrating is a learned skill.
- It takes a while to build up the ability and stamina to narrate.
- Don't be discouraged if your child complains when you ask for narration.
- Complaints at some stage, from a child, about narration is common.
- Narration demands focus and thinking
- It will get easier as time goes by, so keep on persisting.
- Keep narration times very short.

If you are like me you might get bored while you wait for your child to slowly and laboriously narrate to you. My solution was to knit! Actually, I also taught my children to knit. So they knitted while I read to them and this kept them focused on keeping still and listening to me. Then I knitted while they narrated back to me.

Remember the immense value of narration to your child in making him an active responsible party in the learning process.

NARRATIONS WORK WITH MORE THAN ONE CHILD

If your children are all nine or under, then you will probably be reading aloud and asking for oral narrations with more than one child. In this case, you can warn the children that you will be asking for a narration at the end of the reading but don't say who you will ask. This way, all the children need to be attentive and prepared. This is the way it worked in Charlotte Mason's schools where a whole class would be ready to narrate.

Actually, I tend to give the first turn of narrating to the youngest child listening, as they are most likely to have the least to say. Then you can give the older children an opportunity to add something to the narration, working through the children to the oldest child. This way all the children get the chance to shine.

If you have older children, they will be doing their own silent reading and their own written narrations. Often, people get overwhelmed with all the books involved in a Charlotte Mason education, but it's important to remember that once a child can read, he will be doing his own reading. This will free you to work with younger children.

SUMMARY

In this chapter I have told you about narration, which is a cornerstone of teaching using Charlotte Mason's ideas. I've talked about the great value of narration in the teaching process. And I've explained how and why this very simple-sounding concept is actually much richer and more useful than it first appears.

I've addressed some common problems that people have when teaching narration, and I've given you a stack of tips and techniques for dealing with those problems. Hopefully, these tools will help you to succeed in teaching this wonderful skill to your children.

And now that you understand how valuable the skill of narration is to your child, you will be encouraged to persist in teaching your child to narrate.

ASSIGNMENT

- Ask your child for a narration. Think carefully about how you will do it. Try to make it casual and informal if you can, although you will have thought it through and prepared yourself. Basically, it's you learning the lesson of how to ask for and listen to a narration, rather than your child learning to narrate.
- Watch out for any impromptu narrations that you receive from your children.
- Read what Charlotte Mason had to say about narration. Volume 1, page 232 -233, page 289 and vol 3 pages 179—181

SUPPLEMENT

QUOTATIONS FROM THE ORIGINAL HOMESCHOOL SERIES BY CHARLOTTE MASON

Volume 1, page 232 -233

...our business for the moment is with what children under nine can narrate.

Method of Lesson.— In every case the reading should be consecutive from a well-chosen book. Before the reading for the day begins, the teacher should talk a little (and get the children to talk) about the last lesson, with a few words about what is to be read, in order that the children may be animated by expectation; but she should beware of explanation and, especially, of forestalling the narrative.

Then, she may read two or three pages, enough to include an episode; after that, let her call upon the children to narrate,— in turns, if there be several of them. They not only narrate with spirit and accuracy, but succeed in catching the style of their author.

It is not wise to tease them with corrections; they may begin with an endless chain of 'ands,' but they soon leave this off, and their narrations become good enough in style and composition to be put in a 'print book'! This sort of narration lesson should not occupy more than a quarter of an hour.

The book should always be deeply interesting, and when the narration is over, there should be a little talk in which moral points are brought out, pictures shown to illustrate the lesson, or diagrams drawn on the blackboard.

As soon as children are able to read with ease and fluency, they read their own lesson, either aloud or silently, with a view to narration; but where it is necessary to make omissions, as in the Old Testament narratives and Plutarch's Lives, for example, it is better that the teacher should always read the lesson which is to be narrated.

Volume 1, page 289

Indeed, it is most interesting to hear children of seven or eight go through a long story without missing a detail, putting every event in its right order. These narrations are never a slavish reproduction of the original. A child's individuality plays about what he enjoys, and the story comes from his lips, not precisely as the author tells it, but with a certain spirit and colouring which express the narrator.

By the way, it is very important that children should be allowed to narrate in their own way, and should not be pulled up or helped with words and expressions from the text.

A narration should be original as it comes from the child—that is, his own mind should have acted upon the matter it has received.

Narrations which are mere feats of memory are quite valueless.

Volume 3, page 88

I think it would be well if the habit of narration were more encouraged, in place of written composition. On the whole, it is more useful to be able to speak than to write, and the man or woman who is able to do the former can generally do the latter.

Volume 3 Pages 179—181

Value of Narration.— The simplest way of dealing with a paragraph or a chapter is to require the child to narrate its contents after a single attentive reading,—one reading, however slow, should be made a condition; for we are all too apt to make sure we shall have another opportunity of finding out 'what 'tis all about' There is the chapterly review if we fail to get a clear grasp of the news of the day; and, if we fail a second time, there is a monthly or a quarterly review or an annual summing up: in fact, many of us let present-day history pass by us with easy minds, feeling sure that, in the end, we shall be compelled to see the bearings of events. This is a bad habit to get into; and we should do well to save our children by not giving them the vague expectation of second and third and tenth opportunities to do that which should have been done at first.

A Single Careful Reading.— There is much difference between intelligent reading, which the pupil should do in silence, and a mere parrot-like cramming up of contents; and it is not a bad test of education to be able to give the points of a description, the sequence of a series of incidents, the links in a chain of argument, correctly, after a single careful reading.

This is a power which a barrister, a publisher, a scholar, labours to acquire; and it is a power which children can acquire with great ease, and once acquired, the gulf is bridged which divides the reading from the non-reading community.

Other Ways of using Books.— But this is only one way to use books: others are to enumerate the statements in a given paragraph or chapter; to analyse a chapter, to divide it into paragraphs under proper headings, to tabulate and classify series; to trace cause to consequence and consequence to cause; to discern character and perceive how character and circumstance interact; to get lessons of life and conduct, or the living knowledge which makes for science, out of books; all this is possible for school boys and girls, and until they have begun to use books for themselves in such ways, they can hardly be said to have begun their education.

The Teacher's Part.— The teacher's part is, in the first place, to see what is to be done, to look over the of the day in advance and see what mental discipline, as well as what vital knowledge, this and that lesson afford; and then to set such questions and such tasks as shall give full scope to his pupils' mental activity.

Let marginal notes be freely made, as neatly and beautifully as may be, for books should be handled with reverence. Let numbers, letters, underlining be used to help the eye and to save the needless fag of writing abstracts. Let the pupil write for himself half a dozen questions which cover the passage studied; he need not write the answers if he be taught that the mind can know nothing but what it can produce in the form of an answer to a question put by the mind to itself.

Disciplinary Devices must not come between Children and the Soul of the Book.— These few hints by no means cover the disciplinary uses of a good school-book; but let us be careful that our disciplinary devices, and our mechanical devices to secure and tabulate the substance of knowledge, do not come between the children and that which is the soul of the book, the living thought it contains.

Science is doing so much for us in these days, nature is drawing so close to us, art is unfolding so much meaning to us, the world is becoming so rich for us, that we are a little in danger of neglecting the art of deriving sustenance from books.

Let us not in such wise impoverish our lives and the lives of our *children; for, to quote the golden words of Milton: "Books are not absolutely dead things, but do contain a potency of life in them to be as active as that soul was, whose progeny they are; nay, they do preserve, as in a vial, the purest efficacy and extraction of that living intellect that bred them.*

As good almost kill a man, as kill a good book; who kills a man kills a good reasonable creature, God's image; but he who destroys a good book, kills reason itself - kills the image of God, as it were, in the eye."

Volume 5, page 305

Therefore it is well that children should, at any rate, have the outlet of narration, that they should tell the things they know in full detail; and, when the humour takes them, 'play' the persons, act the scenes

Volume 6, page 17

...if it is desirable to ask questions in order to emphasize certain points, these should be asked after and not before, or during, the act of narration.

CHAPTER 7.
OUTDOOR EDUCATION

In this chapter we are going to look at the subject of outdoor education and see what Charlotte Mason had to say about it and if or why she considered it to be important.

WHAT IS OUTDOOR EDUCATION?

Outdoor education is simply the child being outside, and learning, playing, observing, and gathering information along the way.

Charlotte Mason believed that children under the age of nine should spend as much time as possible out of doors.

Here's a quotation from Volume 1, pages 44 – 45, that I recommend you read really carefully:

'I make a point, says a judicious mother, 'of sending my children out, weather permitting, for an hour in the winter, and two hours a day in the summer months.'

That is well; but it is not enough. In the first place, do not send them; if it is anyway possible, take them; for, although the children should be left much to themselves, there is a great deal to be done and a great deal to be prevented during these long hours in the open air. And long hours they should be; Not two, but four, five, or six hours they should have on every tolerably fine day, from April till October. …

They must be let alone, left to themselves a great deal, to take in what they can of the beauty of earth and heavens; for of the evils of modern education few are worse than this—that the perpetual cackle of his elders leaves the poor child not a moment of time, nor an inch of space, wherein to wonder- and grow.

At the same time, here is the mother's opportunity to train the seeing eye, the hearing ear, and to drop seeds of truth into the open soul of the child, which shall germinate, blossom, and bear fruit, without further help or knowledge of hers. Then, there is much to be got by perching in a tree or nestling in heather, but muscular development comes of more active ways, and an hour or two should be spent in vigorous play; and last, and truly least, a lesson or two must be got in.

Obviously, you can see from this excerpt that Charlotte Mason put a huge store on the children being outside, playing and learning.

I find this excerpt even more interesting when I put it into context. Charlotte Mason wrote this when she lived in Bradford in the north of England. She taught it to her students in Ambleside, in the north-west of England.

And the climate in Bradford and Ambleside is not warm, dry, and comfortable.

I was brought up 80 km from Ambleside and have been there countless times. I know what it's like. It rains a lot, the air is damp, and it can be quite cool, even in summer.

In winter, daytime temperature highs would be in high single figures Centigrade. The children would not have thermal underwear and modern waterproof clothes.

In summer time the weather can be warm one day, cool the next day, with a guarantee of 'unpredictable'.

What I want to get across to you is that Charlotte Mason was advocating that children play and be outside, even in inclement and cool weather. For several hours a day, seven months of the year, plus some.

We all agree that the pressures and the comforts of our modern lifestyle mean that we can be totally insulated from the weather. For example, I can go to the mall or the library on a cold winter's day when it's pouring down with rain, and I don't need a coat or an umbrella. In fact, I can go to the mall or the library without putting my foot on wet ground. I have an 'internal access' garage and I can park in the undercover car park at the mall or the library.

So do Charlotte Mason's ideas on this topic still hold relevance today? Or are they too hard to incorporate into a modern homeschooling lifestyle?

I think we can apply this idea in an easy, simple way...

MODERN DAY OUTDOOR PLAY

What would Charlotte Mason say if she came to visit me? I think she might tell me to wrap the children up warmly and send them .... eeek! No! I mean take them outdoors to play.

She wouldn't be worrying about a bit of wind or a spot of rain or a touch of sunshine. She would also suggest that I don't bore my children with 'perpetual cackle' from me but allow them to make their own connections and discoveries. This means that we, the parents, don't talk incessantly to our children, explaining, questioning, and lecturing. We just allow the children to enjoy the outdoors.

HOW WILL THIS WORK IN MODERN HOMESCHOOLING LIFE?

In a hot climate, I see the children going out to play before or after breakfast – before it gets too hot in summer. And in a cold climate, for a short time, so that the children won't get too cold in winter.

What if you live in a place which has blizzards? Well obviously, you aren't going to take or send children out to play when it's really cold or wet or blowing a gale. On a very cold or hot day the children can play outside for short bursts, several times a day.

If you have a wide age range of children, then send the young ones out for morning tea play time earlier than the older ones. This gives them a longer playtime and it gives you a few extra minutes with an older child. Make sure you are sitting where you can see and/or hear the little ones playing, so that you know they are safe, but no need to cosset them.

The same play time will happen again at lunch time, and then again in the late afternoon. These long play times will satisfy the children, give them exercise, allow them to relate to each other and to nature. You will get visits from them with insects, bits of plants etc, and I'll show you how to make the best use of those 'visits' in the next chapter.

So I hope the pressure is off there. No need to take your child out for hours each day, but they will get lots of constructive outdoor play time.

I urge you to read that quotation at the beginning of this chapter again; read it really carefully, and listen to what Charlotte Mason is suggesting.

DISCOVERING NATURE

Charlotte Mason believed that children should become familiar with the things they see in their own neighbourhood—what trees, what flowers, what birds, what insects? They should recognise an anthill, a dandelion, a sparrow, a blackbird, local trees, birds, insects, weeds and wildflowers...

Here in New Zealand, the list might include things like a weta, a tui, a tea-tree, a kauri, a kowhai.

Wherever you are, I know you would quickly make up a list of local wildlife and plant life.

And then she writes, in Volume 5, page 166

I should think most of 'our' mothers would feel disgraced if her child of six were not able to recognise any ordinary British tree from a twig with leaf-buds only. It's Nature's lore, and the children take to it like ducks to the water; the first six or seven years of their lives are spent out of doors—in possible weather—learning this sort of thing, instead of pottering over picture-books and A B C.

I absolutely love this quotation! - 'instead of pottering over picture books and ABC'!

That is certainly counter cultural and a huge challenge for us, isn't it?

SUMMARY

In this chapter we have looked at what Charlotte Mason had to say about Outdoor Education. I've given you a couple of quotations from her. I've also tried to help you see that outdoor education isn't as hard or as complicated as some people have thought it is, and you can make it work in your family for some if not most of the year.

ASSIGNMENT

The challenge Charlotte Mason gives us on the subject of outdoor education is so interesting. Read some more about outdoor education:
- Volume 1, page 29 and pages 42 – 50

SUPPLEMENT

Quotations from The Original Homeschool Series by Charlotte Mason

Volume 1, page 29

The Children Walk every Day.—'The children walk every day; they are never out less than an hour when the weather is suitable.' That is better than nothing; so is this: An East London school mistress notices the pale looks of one of her best girls.

"Have you had any dinner, Nellie?"

"Ye-es" (with hesitation).

"What have you had?"

"Mother gave Jessie and me a halfpenny to buy our dinners, and we bought a haporth of aniseed drops- they go further than bread"—with an appeal in her eyes against possible censure for extravagance.

Children do not develop at their best upon aniseed drops for dinner, nor upon an hour's 'constitutional' daily. Possibly science will bring home to us more and more the fact that animal life, pent under cover, is supported under artificial conditions, just as is plant life in a glass house.

Volume 1, pages 42 - 50

OUT-OF-DOOR LIFE FOR THE CHILDREN

Meals out of Doors.—People who live in the country know the value of fresh air very well, and their children live out of doors, with intervals within for sleeping and eating. As to the latter, even country people do not make full use of their opportunities.

On fine days when it is warm enough to sit out with wraps, why should not tea and breakfast, everything but a hot dinner, be served out of doors? For we are an overwrought generation, running to nerves as a cabbage runs to seed; and every hour spent in the open is a clear gain, tending to the increase of brain power and bodily vigour, and to the lengthening of life itself.

They who know what it is to have fevered skin and throbbing brain deliciously soothed by the cool touch of the air are inclined to make a new rule of life, Never be within doors when you can rightly be without.

Besides, the gain of an hour or two in the open air, there is this to be considered: meals taken al fresco are usually joyous, and there is nothing like gladness for converting meat and drink into healthy blood and tissue.

All the time, too, the children are storing up memories of a happy childhood. Fifty years hence they will see the shadows of the boughs making patterns on the white tablecloth; and sunshine, children's laughter, hum of bees, and scent of flowers are being bottled up for after refreshment.

For Dwellers in Towns and Suburbs.—But it is only the people who live, so to speak, in their own gardens who can make a practice of giving their children tea out of doors. For the rest of us, and the most of us, who live in towns or the suburbs of towns, that is included in the larger question—How much time daily in the open air should the children have? And how is it possible to secure this for them?

In this time of extraordinary pressure, educational and social, perhaps a mother's first duty to her children is to secure for them a quiet growing time, a full six years of passive receptive life, the waking part of it spent for the most part out in the fresh air. And this, not for the gain in bodily health alone—body and soul, heart and mind, are nourished with food convenient for them when the children are let alone, let to live without friction and without stimulus amongst happy influences which incline them to be good.

Possibilities of a Day in the Open.—I make a point, says a judicious mother, of sending my children out, weather permitting, for an hour in the winter, and two hours a day in the summer months. That is well; but it is not enough.

In the first place, do not send them; if it is anyway possible, take them; for, although the children should be left much to themselves, there is a great deal to be done and a great deal to be prevented during these long hours in the open air. And long hours they should be; Not two, but four, five, or six hours they should have on every tolerably fine day, from April till October.

Impossible! Says an overwrought mother who sees her way to no more for her children than a daily hour or so on the pavements of the neighbouring London squares. Let me repeat, that I venture to suggest, not what is practicable in any household, but what seems to me absolutely best for the children; and that, in the faith that mothers work wonders once they are convinced that wonders are demanded of them.

A journey of twenty minutes by rail or omnibus, and a luncheon basket, will make a day in the country possible to most town dwellers; and if one day, why not many, even every suitable day?

Supposing we have got them, what is to be done with these golden hours, so that every one shall be delightful? They must be spent with some method, or the mother will be taxed and the children bored.

There is a great deal to be accomplished in this large fraction of the children's day. They must be kept in a joyous temper all the time, or they will miss some of the strengthening and refreshing held in charge for them by the blessed air. They must be let alone, left to themselves a great deal, to take in what they can of the beauty of earth and heavens; for of the evils of modern education few are worse than this—that the perpetual cackle of his elders leaves the poor child not a moment of time, nor an inch of space, wherein to wonder—and grow.

At the same time, here is the mother's opportunity to train the seeing eye, the hearing ear, and to drop seeds of truth into the open soul of the child, which shall germinate, blossom, and bear fruit, without further help or knowledge of hers. Then, there is much to be got by perching in a tree or nestling in heather, but muscular development comes of more active ways, and an hour or two should be spent in vigorous play; and last, and truly least, a lesson or two must be got in.

No Story-Books.—Let us suppose mother and children arrived at some breezy open wherein it seemeth always afternoon. In the first place, it is not her business to entertain the little people: there should be no story-books, no telling of tales, as little talk as possible, and that to some purpose. Who thinks to amuse children with tale or talk at a circus or pantomime? And here, is there not infinitely more displayed for their delectation?

Our wise mother, arrived, first sends the children to let off their spirits in a wild scamper, with cry; hallo, and hullaballo, and any extravagance that comes into their young heads. There is no distinction between big and little; the latter love to follow in the wake of their elders, and, in lessons or play, to pick up and do according to their little might.

As for the baby, he is in bliss: divested of his garments, he kicks and crawls, and clutches the grass, laughs soft baby laughter, and takes in his little knowledge of shapes and properties in his own wonderful fashion—clothed in a woollen gown, long and loose, which is none the worse for the worst usage it may get.

II.—SIGHT-SEEING

By-and-by the others come back to their mother, and, while wits are fresh and eyes are keen, she sends them off on an exploring expedition—Who can see the most, and tell the most, about yonder hillock or Brook, hedge, or copse. This is an exercise that delights children, and may be endlessly varied, carried on in the spirit of a game, and yet with the exactness and carefulness of a lesson.

How to See.—Find out all you can about that cottage at the foot of the hill; but do not pray about too much. Soon they are back, and there is a crowd of excited faces, and a hubbub of tongues, and random observations are shot breathlessly into the mother's ear.

There are bee-hives. We saw a lot of bees going into one.

There is a long garden. Yes, and there are sunflowers in it.

And hen-and-chicken daisies and pansies.

And there's a great deal of pretty blue flowers with rough leaves, mother; what do you suppose it is?

Borage for the bees, most likely; they are very fond of it.

Oh, and there are apple and pear and plum trees on one side; there's a little path up the middle, you know.

On which hand side are the fruit trees? The right—no, the left; let me see, which is my thimble-hand? Yes, it is the right-hand side.

And there are potatoes and cabbages, and mint and things on the other side.

Where are the flowers, then? Oh, they are just the borders, running down each side of the path.

But we have not told mother about the wonderful apple tree; I should think there are a million apples on it, all ripe and rosy!

A million, Fanny?

Well, a great many, mother; I don't know how many.

And so on, indefinitely; the mother getting by degrees a complete description of the cottage and its garden.

Educational Uses of Sight-Seeing.—This is all play to the children, but the mother is doing invaluable work; she is training their powers of observation and expression, increasing their vocabulary and their range of ideas by giving them the name and the uses of an object at the right moment,—when they ask, What is it? And What is it for? And she is training her children in truthful habits, by making them careful to see the fact and to state it exactly, without omission or exaggeration.

The child who describes, A tall tree, going up into a point, with rather roundish leaves; not a pleasant tree for shade, because the branches all go up, deserves to learn the name of the tree, and anything her mother has to tell her about it. But the little bungler, who fails to make it clear whether he is describing an elm or a beech, should get no encouragement; not a foot should his mother move to see his tree, no coaxing should draw her into talk about it, until, in despair, he goes off, and comes back with some more certain note—rough or smooth bark, rough or smooth leaves,—then the mother considers, pronounces, and, full of glee, he carries her off to see for himself.

Discriminating Observation.—By degrees the children will learn discriminatingly every feature of the landscapes with which they are familiar; and think what a delightful possession for old age and middle life is a series of pictures imaged, feature by feature, in the sunny glow of the child's mind! The miserable thing about the childish recollections of most persons is that they are blurred, distorted, incomplete, no more pleasant to look upon than a fractured cup or a torn garment; and the reason is, not that the old scenes are forgotten, but that they were never fully seen.

At the time, there was no more than a hazy impression that such and such objects were present, and naturally, after a lapse of years those features can rarely be recalled of which the child was not cognisant when he saw them before him.

III.—PICTURE-PAINTING

Method of.—So exceedingly delightful is this faculty of taking mental photographs, exact images, of the beauties of Nature we go about the world for the refreshment of seeing, that it is worthwhile to exercise children in another way towards this end, bearing in mind, however, that they see the near and the minute, but can only be made with an effort to look at the wide and the distant.

Get the children to look well at some patch of landscape, and then to shut their eyes and call up the picture before them, if any bit of it is blurred, they had better look again. When they have a perfect image before their eyes, let them say what they see.

Thus: I see a pond; it is shallow on this side, but deep on the other; trees come to the waters edge on that side, and you can see their green leaves and branches so plainly in the water that you would think there was a wood underneath. Almost touching the trees in the water is a bit of blue sky with a soft white cloud; and when you look up you see that same little cloud, ,but with a great deal of sky instead of a patch, because there are no trees up there. There are lovely little water-lilies round the far edge of the pond, and two or three of the big round leaves are turned up like sails. Near where I am standing three cows have come to drink, and one has got far into the water, nearly up to her neck, etc.

Strain on the Attention.—This, too, is an exercise children delight in, but, as it involves some strain on the attention, it is fatiguing, and should only be employed now and then. It is, however, well worthwhile to give children the habit of getting a bit of landscape by heart in this way, because it is the effort of recalling and reproducing that is fatiguing; while the altogether pleasurable act of seeing, fully and in detail, is likely to be repeated unconsciously until it becomes a habit by the child who is required now and then to reproduce what he sees.

Seeing Fully and in Detail.—At first the children will want a little help in the art of seeing. The mother will say, Look at the reflection of the trees! There might be a wood under the water. What do those standing up leaves remind you of? And so on, until the children have noticed the salient points of the scene.

She will even herself learn off two or three scenes, and describe them with closed eyes for the children's amusement; and such little mimics are they, and at the same time so sympathetic, that any graceful fanciful touch which she throws into her descriptions will be reproduced with variations in theirs.

The children will delight in this game of picture-painting all the more if the mother introduce it by describing some great picture gallery she has seen—pictures of mountains, of moors, of stormy seas, of ploughed fields, of little children at play, of an old woman knitting,—and goes on to say, that though she does not paint her pictures on canvas and have them put in frames, she carries about with her just such a picture gallery; for whenever she sees anything lovely or interesting, she looks at it until she has the picture in her mind's eye; and then she carries it away with her, her own for ever, a picture on view just when she wants it.

A Means of After-Solace and Refreshment.—It would be difficult to overrate this habit of seeing and storing as a means of after-solace and refreshment. The busiest of us have holidays when we slip our necks out of the yoke and come face to face with Nature, to be healed and blessed by

The breathing balm,
The silence and the calm
 Of mute, insensate things.

This immediate refreshment is open to everybody according to his measure; but it is a mistake to suppose that everybody is able to carry away a refreshing image of that which gives him delight. Only a few can say with Wordsworth, of scenes they have visited

Though absent long,
These forms of beauty have not been to me
As is a landscape to a blind man's eye;
But oft, in lonely rooms, and mid the din
Of towns and cities, I have owed to them,
In hours of weariness, sensations sweet,
Felt in the blood, and felt along the heart;
And passing even into my purer mind,
With tranquil restoration.

And yet this is no high poetic gift which the rest of us must be content to admire, but a common reward for taking pains in the act of seeing which parents may do a great deal to confer upon their children.

The mother must beware how she spoils the simplicity, the objective character of the child's enjoyment, by treating his little descriptions as feats of cleverness to be repeated to his father or to visitors; she had better make a vow to suppress herself, 'to say nothing to nobody,' in his presence at any rate, though the child should show himself a born poet.

CHAPTER 8.
NATURE WALKS AND NATURE TABLES

Charlotte Mason believed in taking all children for nature walks. She said:

It seems to me a sine quâ non [an essential ingredient] *of a living education that all school children of whatever grade should have one half-day in the week, throughout the year, in the fields. There are few towns where country of some sort is not accessible, and every child should have the opportunity of watching from week to week, the procession of the seasons.* Volume 3, page 237

They [Nature walks] *lay up that store of 'common information' which Huxley considered should precede science teaching; and, what is much more important, they learn to know and delight in natural objects as in the familiar faces of friends.* Volume 3, page 237

Often people see Charlotte Mason's philosophy of education as passing over the sciences and concentrating solely on the arts, when in actual fact she was laying a very strong deep foundation for good science study.

In volume 6 she says:

'Scientific truths,' said Descartes,' are battles won.' Describe to the young the principal and most heroic of these battles; you will thus interest them in the results of science and you will develop in them a scientific spirit by means of the enthusiasm for the conquest of truth. . . .

How interesting Arithmetic and Geometry might be if we gave a short history of their principal theorems, if the child were meant to be present at the labours of a Pythagoras, a Plato, a Euclid, or in modern times, of a Descartes, a Pascal, or a Leibnitz.

Great theories instead of being lifeless and anonymous abstractions would become living human truths each with its own history like a statue by Michael Angelo or like a painting by Raphael.

I really like this passage. I think about it a lot. And I especially like that first sentence: 'Scientific truths,' said Descartes,' are battles won.'

This is so true, isn't it? Once we have a scientific truth in something like medicine, or in engineering, or whatever, it's a battle won. What a great thought!

And it starts with nature walks and being outdoors a lot for children.

I sometimes wonder what Charlotte Mason would think about the Discovery Channel and nature programmes. And I don't think she would be as enthusiastic about them as some people are. It hit home to me at the millennium celebrations in 2000 when I heard that people were indoors, watching people watching the sun rise on their television screens, instead of outdoors watching the real sun rise in the real sky.

It's better to be more familiar with the humble creatures and plants you find in your own back yard than to know a heap about exotic creatures across the world that you have never actually seen in real life. So let's look at how you get familiar with your local nature.

NATURE WALKS AND NATURE JOURNALS

When I was little we always had a nature table in our classroom at school. We had nature books and nature walks. I didn't know it at the time, but this idea came from Charlotte Mason who used nature journals in her teaching. With my own children I also used a nature journal.

HOW TO USE A NATURE JOURNAL

Some people use a spiral bound book and others use a ring binder and single sheets of paper.

- The advantage of a ring binder is that you can use single sheets of paper on a clipboard and add them to your binder as you like. You can leave out pages you don't like and re-order the pages as you like.
- The advantage of the notebook is that you learn to live with all the pages you have done and the finished book can look very beautiful.
- Some people use coloured pencils in their illustrations. They take their nature journals with

them when they go out on a trip and they add something to their books a couple of times a week or month.

HOW TO START USING YOUR NATURE JOURNAL

A good way to present the idea of nature journals to the children for the first time is to get a drawing book for yourself as well as for the children. Then you set the example by drawing.

- Start with a tree in your back yard or neighbourhood. Start talking about it: ask, do you know what sort of tree it is?
- Pick a leaf, settle down to draw.
- Look it up in your field guide, find its Latin name, what is its local name?
- Keep in mind that this is not an art lesson and the results of the drawing are not for criticism or display. This is a lesson in observation.
- Over the weeks, continue to draw whatever you have around the house and garden. You could draw all the plants in your yard, all the insects that come into the house and all the bugs and creepy crawlies that you see round the section.
- As the years go by the children will develop a knowledge of nature and the nature notebook will become a treasured possession, recording all sorts of exciting discoveries and golden moments.

HOW TO MAKE A NATURE TABLE

I always kept a nature table in our house. I used a low bookshelf top for display, and included all sorts of scientific discoveries; we have had an Archimedes Screw, an Egyptian Shaduf, an electrical circuit among other things.

- To start you could plan a walk to look for signs of the season, bring treasures home (careful not to damage anything) and display your treasures on a little table or cupboard-top.
- Change the display regularly, put out some of the treasures you have collected on your walk.

- Take another walk along the same route a week later and another a week later.
- Choose a park with deciduous trees. Each week the children will observe the signs of the season
- Have tadpoles in spring, caterpillars in summer, autumn leaves in autumn.
- Make labels for things using bright coloured card and thick vivid pen.
- Add the Latin and local names to the labels.
- If you live near the beach, a trip to the beach can be very educational, look at your beach field guide before you go, or take it with you. We used *What's On The Beach?* by Glenys Stace. It is filled with photographs, which make identification easy. The maps and line drawings are easy to understand and go well with the descriptions.
- You can display your beach finds in glass jars filled with water, on your nature table, and don't forget the labels, of course.
- Insects and small animals found in the garden and yard become fascinating when you learn something of their lifecycles and habits. Did you know, for instance that those pretty praying mantises are extremely ferocious and even cannibalistic? Or those ugly earwigs are very good mothers?
- Treasures found by your child in your back yard at play time can be labelled and go on the nature table.
- Have a magnifier at the nature table too, so that things can be examined in detail very easily.

SUMMARY

In this chapter we have looked at how Charlotte Mason introduced teaching science to younger children. We've looked at nature walks, nature journals and nature studies.

ASSIGNMENT

- Try to find out about places to go for walks in your area.
- Consider how you can incorporate outdoor play time and maybe a weekly nature walk into your life with the children.
- Look upon this as a treat and not a chore. Remember to relax and enjoy this time with your children. Record here what you did to relax and enjoy your children.
- Spend some time browsing through the library for books to try out before buying.
- You can look in the Dewey system under 577, 578 and 595 for nature guides and natural history books.
- Look under 919 for walking guides. Look for some local gardening magazines.
- Some reading for this chapter on: OUTDOOR EDUCATION AND NATURE STUDIES: Volume 1 Part II pages 51 – 72. Volume 3 pages 236, 237 & 238

SUPPLEMENT

Volume 1, pages 51 -72

IV. FLOWERS AND TREES

Children should know Field-crops.—In the course of this 'sight-seeing' and 'picture-painting,' opportunities will occur to make the children familiar with rural objects and employments. If there are farm-lands within reach, they should know meadow and pasture, clover, turnip, and corn field, under every aspect, from the ploughing of the land to the getting in of the crops.

Field Flowers and the Life-History of Plants.—Milkwort, eyebright, rest-harrow, lady's-bedstraw, willow-herb, every wild flower that grows in their neighbourhood, they should know quite well; should be able to describe the leaf—its shape, size, growing from the root or from the stem; the manner of flowering—a head of flowers, a single flower, a spike, etc.

And, having made the acquaintance of a wild flower, so that they can never forget it or mistake it, they should examine the spot where they find it, so that they will know for the future in what sort of ground to look for such and such a flower. 'We should find wild thyme here!' 'Oh, this is the very spot for marsh marigolds; we must come here in the spring.' If the mother is no great botanist, she will find Miss Ann Pratt's Wild Flowers [see Appendix A] very useful, with its coloured plates, like enough to identify the flowers, by common English names, and pleasant facts and fancies that the children delight in.

To make collections of wild flowers for the several months, press them, and mount them neatly on squares of cartridge paper, with the English name, habitat, and date of finding each, affords much happy occupation and, at the same time, much useful training: better still is it to accustom children to make careful brush drawings for the flowers that interest them, of the whole plant where possible.

The Study of Trees.—Children should be made early intimate with the trees, too; should pick out half a dozen trees, oak, elm, ash, beech, in their winter nakedness, and take these to be their year-long friends. In the winter, they will observe the light tresses of the birch, the knotted arms of the oak, the sturdy growth of the sycamore. They may wait to learn the names of the trees until the leaves come.

By-and-by, as the spring advances, behold a general stiffening and look of life in the still bare branches; life stirs in the beautiful mystery of the leaf-buds, a nest of delicate baby leaves lying in downy warmth within many waterproof wrappings; oak and elm, beech and birch, each has its own way of folding and packing its leaflets; observe the 'ruby budded lime' and the ash, with its pretty stag's foot of a bud, not green but black—

"More black than ash-buds in the front of March."

The Seasons should be followed.—*But it is hard to keep pace with the wonders that unfold themselves in the 'bountiful season bland.' There are the dangling catkins and the little ruby eyed pistil-late flowers of the hazel—clusters of flowers, both of them, two sorts on a single tree; and the downy staminate catkins of the willow; and the festive breaking out of all the trees into lovely leafage; the learning the patterns of the leaves as they come out, and the naming of the trees from this and other signs.*

Then the flowers come, each shut up tight in the dainty casket we call a bud, as cunningly wrapped as the leaves in their buds, but less carefully guarded, for these 'sweet nurslings' delay their coming for the most part until earth has a warm bed to offer, and the sun a kindly welcome.

Leigh Hunt on Flowers.—*"Suppose," says Leigh Hunt, "suppose flowers themselves were new! Suppose they had just come into the world, a sweet reward for some new goodness... Imagine what we should feel when we saw the first lateral stem bearing off from the main one, and putting forth a leaf. How we should watch the leaf gradually unfolding its little graceful hand; then another, then another; then the main stalk rising and producing more; then one of them giving indications of the astonishing novelty—a bud! then this mysterious bud gradually unfolding like the leaf, amazing us, enchanting us, almost alarming us with delight, as if we knew not what enchantment were to ensue, till at length, in all its fairy beauty, and odorous voluptuousness, and the mysterious elaboration of tender and living sculpture, shines forth the blushing flower." The flowers, it is true, are not new; but the children are; and it is the fault of their elders if every new flower they come upon is not to them a Picciola, a mystery of beauty to be watched from day to day with unspeakable awe and delight.*

Meanwhile, we have lost sight of those half-dozen forest-

trees which the children have taken into a sort of comradeship for the year. Presently they have the delight of discovering that the great trees have flowers, too, flowers very often of the same hue as their leaves, and that some trees have put off having their leaves until their flowers have come and gone. By-and-by there is the fruit, and the discovery that every tree- with exceptions which they need not learn yet—and every plant bears fruit, 'fruit and seed after his kind.'

All this is stale knowledge to older people, but one of the secrets of the educator is to present nothing as stale knowledge, but to put himself in the position of the child, and wonder and admire with him; for every common miracle which the child sees with his own eyes makes of him for the moment another Newton.

Calendars.—It is a capital plan for the children to keep a calendar—the first oak-leaf, the first tadpole, the first cowslip, the first catkin, the first ripe blackberries, where seen, and when. The next year they will know when and where to look out for their favourites, and will, every year, be in a condition to add new observations. Think of the zest and interest, the object, which such a practice will give to daily walks and little excursions. There is hardly a day when some friend may not be expected to hold a first 'At Home.'

Nature Diaries.—As soon as he is able to keep it himself, a nature-diary is a source of delight to a child. Every day's walk gives him something to enter: three squirrels in a larch tree, a jay flying across such a field, a caterpillar climbing up a nettle, a snail eating a cabbage leaf, a spider dropping suddenly to the ground, where he found ground ivy, how it was growing and what plants were growing with it, how bindweed or ivy manages to climb.

Innumerable matters to record occur to the intelligent child. While he is quite young (five or six), he should begin to illustrate his notes freely with brush drawings; he should have a little help at first in mixing colours, in the way of principles, not directions. He should not be told to use now this and now that, but, 'we get purple by mixing so and so,' and then he should be left to himself to get the right tint.

As for drawing, instruction has no doubt its time and place; but his nature diary should be left to his own initiative. A child of six will produce a dandelion, poppy, daisy, iris, with its leaves, impelled by the desire to represent what he sees, with surprising vigour and correctness.

An exercise book with stiff covers serves for a nature diary, but care is necessary in choosing paper that answers both for writing and brush drawing.

'I can't stop thinking.'—But I can't stop thinking; I can't make my mind to sit down!' Poor little girl! All children owe you thanks for giving voice to their dumb woes. And we grown up people have so little imagination, that we send a little boy with an overactive brain to play by himself in the garden in order to escape the fag of lessons. Little we know how the brain-people swarm in and out and rush about!

"The human (brain) is like a millstone, turning ever round and round;
   If it have nothing else to grind, it must itself be ground."

Set the child to definite work by all means, and give him something to grind. But, pray, let him work with things and not with signs—the things of Nature in their own places, meadow and hedgerow, woods and shore.

V. 'LIVING CREATURES'

Field of Interest and Delight.—Then, as for the 'living creatures,' here is a field of unbounded interest and delight. The domesticated animals are soon taken into kindly fellowship by the little people. Perhaps they live too far from the 'real country' for squirrels and wild rabbits to be more to them than a dream of possible delights. But surely there is a pond within reach—by road or rail—where tadpoles may be caught, and carried home in a bottle, fed, and watched through all their changes—fins disappearing, tails getting shorter and shorter, until at last there is no tail at all, and a pretty pert little frog looks you in the face. Turn up any chance stone, and you may come upon a colony of ants. We have always known that it becomes us to consider their ways and be wise; but now, think of all Lord Avebury has told us to make that twelve-year-old ant of his acquaintance quite a personage.

Then, there are the bees. Some of us may have heard the late Dean Farrar describe that lesson he was present at, on 'How doth the little busy bee'- the teacher bright, but the children not responsive; they took no interest at all in little busy bees. He suspected the reason, and questioning the class, found that not one of them had ever seen a bee. 'Had never seen a bee! Think for a moment,' said he, 'of how much that implies'; and then we were moved by an eloquent picture of the sad child-life from which bees and birds and flowers are all shut out.

But how many children are there who do not live in the slums of London, and yet are unable to distinguish a bee from a wasp, or even a 'humble' from a honey-bee!

Children should be encouraged to Watch.—Children should be encouraged to watch, patiently and quietly, until they learn something of the habits and history of bee, ant, wasp, spider, hairy caterpillar, dragon-fly, and whatever of larger growth comes in their way. 'The creatures never have any habits while I am looking!' a little girl in some story-book is made to complain; but that was her fault; the bright keen eyes with which children are blest were made to see, and see into, the doings of creatures too small for the unaided observation of older people.

Ants may be brought under home observation in the following way: Get two pieces of glass 1 foot square, three strips of glass 11 1/2 inches long, and one strip 11 inches long, these all 1/4 inch wide. The glass must be carefully cut so as to fit exactly. Place the four strips of glass upon one of the sheets of glass and fix in an exact square, leaving a 1/2 inch opening, with seccotine or any good fixer. Get from an ant-hill about twelve ants (the yellow ants are best, as the red are inclined to be quarrelsome), a few eggs, and one queen. The queen will be quite as large as an ordinary ant, and so can be easily seen. Take some of the earth of the ant-hill. Put the earth with your ants and eggs upon the sheet of glass and fix the other sheet above, leaving only the small hole in one corner, made by the shorter strip, which should be stopped with a bit of cotton-wool. The ants will be restless for perhaps forty-eight hours, but will then begin to settle and arrange the earth. Remove the wool plug once a week, and replace it after putting two or three drops of honey on it. Once in three weeks remove the plug to drop in with a syringe about ten drops of water. This will not be necessary in the winter while the ants are asleep. This 'nest' will last for years.

With regard to the horror which some children show of beetle, spider, worm, that is usually a trick picked up from grown-up people. Kingsley's children would run after their 'daddy' with a 'delicious worm,' a 'lovely toad,' a 'sweet beetle' carried tenderly in both hands. There are real antipathies not to be overcome, such as Kingsley's own horror of a spider; but children who are accustomed to hold and admire caterpillars and beetles from their babyhood will not give way to affected horrors.

The child who spends an hour in watching the ways of some new 'grub' he has come upon will be a man of mark yet. Let all he finds out about it be entered in his diary—by his mother, if writing be a labour to him,—where he finds it, what it is doing, or seems to him to be doing; its colour, shape, legs: some day he will come across the name of the creature, and will recognise the description of an old friend.

The Force of Public Opinion in the Home.—Some children are born naturalists, with a bent inherited, perhaps, from an unknown ancestor; but every child has a natural interest in the living things about him which it is the business of his parents to encourage; for, but few children are equal to holding their own in the face of public opinion; and if they see that the things which interest them are indifferent or disgusting to you, their pleasure in them vanishes, and that chapter in the book of Nature is closed to them.

It is likely that the Natural History of Selborne would never have been written had it not been that the naturalist's father used to take his boys on daily foraging expeditions, when not a moving or growing thing, not a pebble nor a boulder within miles of Selborne, escaped their eager examination. Audubon, the American ornithologist, is another instance of the effect of this kind of early training. "When I had hardly learned to walk," he says, "and to articulate those first words always so endearing to parents, the productions of Nature that lay spread all around were constantly pointed out to me...My father generally accompanied my steps, procured birds and flowers for me, and pointed out the elegant movements of the former, the beauty and softness of their plumage, the manifestations of their pleasure, or their sense of danger, and the always perfect forms and splendid attire of the latter. He would speak of the departure and return of the birds with the season, describe their haunts, and, more wonderful than all, their change of livery!

thus exciting me to study them, and to raise my mind towards their great Creator."

What Town Children can Do.—Town children may get a great deal of pleasure in watching the ways of sparrows—knowing little birds, and easily tamed by a dole of crumbs,—and their days out will bring them in the way of new acquaintances.

But much may be done with sparrows. A friend writes:—"Have you seen the man in the gardens of Tuileries feeding and talking to dozens of them? They sit on his hat, his hands, and feed from his fingers. When he raises his arms they all flutter up and then settle again on him and round him. I have watched him call a sparrow from a distance by name and refuse food to all others till 'petit chou,' a pretty pied sparrow, came for his destined bit. Others had their names and came at call, but I could not see any distinguishing feature; and the crowd of sparrows on the walk, benches and railing, formed a most attentive audience to the bright French talk which kept them in constant motion as they were, here one and there another, invited to come for a tempting morsel. Truly a St Francis and the birds!"

The child who does not know the portly form ad spotted breast of the thrush, the graceful flight of the swallow, the yellow bill of the blackbird, the gush of song which the skylark pours from above, is nearly as much to be pitied as those London children who 'had never seen a bee.'

A pleasant acquaintance, easy to pick up, is the hairy caterpillar. The moment to seize him is when he is seen shuffling along the ground in a great hurry; he is on the look-out for quiet quarters in which to lie up: put him in a box, then, and over the box with net, through which you may watch his operations. Food does not matter—he has other things to attend to. By-and-by he spins a sort of white tent or hammock, into which he retires; you may see through it and watch him, perhaps at the very moment when his skin splits asunder, leaving him, for months to come, an egg-shaped mass without any sign of life. At last the living thing within breaks out of this bundle, and there it is, the hand! some tiger-moth, fluttering feeble wings against the net.

Most children of six have had this taste of a naturalist's experience, and it is worth speaking of only because, instead of being merely a harmless amusement, it is a valuable piece of education, of more use to the child than the reading of a whole book of natural history, or much geography and Latin.

For the evil is, that children get their knowledge of natural history, like all their knowledge, at second hand. They are so sated with wonders, that nothing surprises them; and they are so little used to see for themselves, that nothing interests them. The cure for this blasé condition is, to let them alone for a bit, and then begin on new lines. Poor children, it is no fault of theirs if they are not as they were meant to be—curious eager little souls, all agog to explore so much of this wonderful world as they can get at, as quite their first business in life.

"He prayeth best who loveth best
All things both great and small;
For the dear God who loveth us,
He made and loveth all."

Nature Knowledge the most important for Young Children.— It would be well if we all persons in authority, parents and all who act for parents, could make up our minds that there is no sort of knowledge to be got in these early years so valuable to children as that which they get for themselves of the world they live in.

Let them once get touch with Nature, and a habit is formed which will be a source of delight through life. We were all meant to be naturalists, each in his degree, and it is inexcusable to live in a world so full of the marvels of plant and animal life and to care for none of these things.

Mental Training of a Child Naturalist.—Consider, too, what an unequalled mental training the child-naturalist is getting for any study or calling under the sun—the powers of attention, of discrimination, of patient pursuit, growing with his growth, what will they not fit him for? Besides, life is so interesting to him, that he has no time for the faults of temper which generally have their source in ennui; there is no reason why he should be peevish or sulky or obstinate when he is always kept well amused.

Nature Work especially valuable for Girls.—I say 'he' from force of habit, as speaking of the representative sex, but truly that she should be thus conversant with Nature is a matter of infinitely more importance to the little girl: she it is who is most tempted to indulge in ugly tempers (as child and woman) because time hangs heavy on her hands; she, whose idler, more desultory habits of mind want the spur and bridle of an earnest absorbing pursuit; whose feebler health demands to be braced by an out-of-door life full of healthy excitement.

Moreover, is it to the girls, little and big, a most true kindness to lift them out of themselves and out of the round of petty personal interests and emulations which too often hem in their lives; and then, with whom but the girls must it rest to mould the generations yet to be born?

VI.—FIELD-LORE AND NATURALISTS' BOOKS

Reverence for Life.—Is it advisable, then, to teach the children the elements of natural science, of biology, botany, zoology? on the whole, no: the dissection even of a flower is painful to a sensitive child, and, during the first six or eight years of life, I would not teach them any botany which should necessitate the pulling of flowers to bits; much less should they be permitted to injure or destroy any (not noxious) form of animal life.

Reverence for life, as a wonderful and awful gift, which a ruthless child may destroy but never can restore, is a lesson of first importance to the child:—

"Let knowledge grow from more to more;
But more of reverence in us dwell."

The child who sees his mother with reverent touch lift an early snowdrop to her lips, learns a higher lesson than the 'print-books' can teach. Years hence, when the children are old enough to understand that science itself is in a sense sacred and demands some sacrifices, all the 'common information' they have been gathering until then, and the habits of observation they have acquired, will form a capital groundwork for a scientific education. In the meantime, let them consider the lilies of the field and the fowls of the air.

Rough Classification at First Hand.—For convenience in describing they should be able to name and distinguish petals, sepals, and so on; and they should be encouraged to make such rough classifications as they can with their slight knowledge of both animal and vegetable forms.

Plants with heart-shaped or spoon-shaped leaves, with whole or divided leaves; leaves with criss-cross veins and leaves with straight veins; bell-shaped flowers and cross-shaped flowers; flowers with three petals, with four, with five; trees which keep their leaves all the year, and trees which lose them in autumn; creatures with a backbone and creatures without; creatures that eat grass and creatures that eat flesh, and so on.

To make collections of leaves and flowers, pressed and

mounted, and arranged according to their form, affords much pleasure, and, what is better, valuable training in the noticing of differences and resemblances. Patterns for this sort of classification of leaves and flowers will be found in every little book for elementary botany.

The power to classify, discriminate, distinguish between things that differ, is amongst the highest faculties of the human intellect, and no opportunity to cultivate it should be let slip; but a classification got out of books, that the child does not make for himself, cultivates no power but that of verbal memory, and a phrase or two of 'Tamil' or other unknown tongue, learnt off, would serve that purpose just as well.

Uses of 'Naturalists' ' Books.—The real use of naturalists' books at this stage is to give the child delightful glimpses into the world of wonders he lives in, to reveal the sorts of things to be seen by curious eyes, and fill him with desire to make discoveries for himself. There are many [Kingsley's Water Babies and Madam How and Lady Why. All Mrs. Brightwen's books. Miss Buckley's (Mrs. Fisher) 'Eyes and no Eyes' Series. Life and her Children, etc. All Seton-Thompson's books. Long's The School of the Woods, The Little Brother of the Bear. Kearton's Wild Nature's Ways. Living Animals of the World.] to be had, all pleasant reading, many of them written by scientific men, and yet requiring little or no scientific knowledge for the enjoyment.

Mothers and Teachers should know about Nature.—The mother cannot devote herself too much to this kind of reading, not only that she may read tit-bits to her children about matters they have come across, but that she may be able to answer their queries and direct their observations. And not only the mother, but any woman, who is likely ever to spend an hour or two in the society of children, should make herself mistress of this sort of information; the children will adore her for knowing what they want to know, and who knows but she may give its bent for life to some young mind designed to do great things for the world.

VII.—THE CHILD GETS KNOWLEDGE BY MEANS OF HIS SENSES

Nature's Teaching.—Watch a child standing at gaze at some sight new to him—a plough at work, for instance—and you will see he is as naturally occupied as is a babe at the breast; he is, in fact, taking in the intellectual food which the working faculty of his brain at this period requires. In his early years the child is all eyes; he observes, or, more truly, he perceives, calling sight, touch, taste, smell, and hearing to his aid, that he may learn all that is discoverable by him about every new thing that comes under his notice.

Everybody knows how a baby fumbles over with soft little fingers, and carries to his mouth, and bangs that it may produce what sound there is in it, the spoon or doll which supercilious grown-up people give him to 'keep him quiet.' The child is at his lessons, and is learning all about it at a rate utterly surprising to the physiologist, who considers how much is implied in the act of 'seeing,' for instance: that to the infant, as to the blind adult restored to sight, there is at first no difference between a flat picture and a solid body,—that the ideas of form and solidity are not obtained by sight at all, but are the judgments of experience.

Then, think, of the vague passes in the air the little fist makes before it lays hold of the object of desire, and you see how he learns the whereabouts of things, having as yet no idea of direction. And why does he cry for the moon? Why does he crave equally, a horse or a house-fly as an appropriate plaything? Because far and near, large and small, are ideas he has yet to grasp. The child has truly a great deal to do before he is in a condition to 'believe his own eyes'; but Nature teaches so gently, so gradually, so persistently, that he is never overdone, but goes on gathering little stores of knowledge about whatever comes before him.

And this is the process the child should continue for the first few years of his life. Now is the storing time which should be spent in laying up images of things familiar. By-and-by he will have to conceive of things he has never seen: how can he do it except by comparison with things he has seen and knows?

By-and-by he will be called upon to reflect, understand, reason; what material will he have, unless he has a magazine of facts to go upon? The child who has been made to observe how high in the heavens the sun is at noon on a summer's day, how low at noon on a day in mid-winter, is able to conceive of the great heat of the tropics under a vertical sun, and to understand the climate of a place depends greatly upon the mean height the sun reaches above the horizon.

Overpressure.—A great deal has been said lately about the danger of overpressure, of requiring too much mental work from a child of tender years. The danger exists; but lies, not in giving the child too much, but in giving him the wrong thing to do, the sort of work for which the present state of his mental development does not fit him. Who expects a boy in petticoats to lift half a hundredweight? But give the child work that Nature intended for him, and the quantity he can get through with ease is practically unlimited. Whoever saw a child tired of seeing, of examining in his own way, unfamiliar things? This is the sort of mental nourishment for which he has an unbounded appetite, because it is that food of the mind on which, for the present, he is meant to grow.

Object Lessons.—Now, how far is this craving for natural sustenance met? In infant and kindergarten schools, by the object lesson, which is good so far as it goes, but is sometimes like that bean a day on which the Frenchman fed his horse. The child at home has more new things brought under his noticed, if with less method. Neither at home nor at school is much effort made to set before the child the abundant 'feast of eyes' which his needs demand.

A Child learns from 'Things.'—We older people, partly because of our maturer intellect, partly because of our defective education, get most of our knowledge through the medium of words. We set the child to learn in the same way, and find him dull and slow. Why? Because it is only with a few words in common use that he associates a definite meaning; all the rest are no more to him than the vocables of a foreign tongue. But set him face to face with a thing, and he is twenty times as quick as you are in knowledge about it; knowledge of things flies to the mind of a child as steel filings to magnet. And, pari passu with his knowledge of things, his vocabulary grows; for it is a law of the mind that what we know, we struggle to express.

This fact accounts for many of the apparently aimless questions of children; they are in quest, not of knowledge, but of words to express the knowledge they have. Now, consider what a culpable waste of intellectual energy it is to shut up a child, blessed with this inordinate capacity for seeing and knowing, within the four walls of a house, or the dreary streets of a town.

Or suppose that he is let run loose in the country where there is plenty to see, it is nearly as bad to let this great faculty of the child's dissipate itself in random observations for want of method and direction.

The Sense of Beauty comes from Early Contact with Nature.— There is no end to the store of common information, got in such a way that it will never be forgotten, with which an intelligent child may furnish himself before he begins his school career. The boy who can tell you off-hand where to find each of the half-dozen most graceful birches, the three or four finest ash trees in the neighbourhood of his home, has chances in a life a dozen to one compared with the lower, slower intelligence that does not know an elm from an oak—not merely chances of success, but chances of a larger, happier life, for it is curious how certain feelings are linked with the mere observation of Nature and natural objects. "The aesthetic sense of the beautiful," says Dr. Carpenter, "of the sublime, of the harmonious, seems in its most elementary form to connect itself immediately with the Perceptions which arise of out of the contact of our minds with external Nature"; !while he quotes Dr. Morrell, who says still more forcibly that "All those who have shown a remarkable appreciation of form and beauty date their first impressions from a period lying far behind the existence of definite ideas or verbal instruction."

Most Grown Men lose the Habit of Observation.—Thus, we owe something to Mr. Evans for taking his little daughter Mary Anne with him on his long business drives among the pleasant Warwickshire lanes; the little girl stood up between her father's knees, seeing much and saying little; and the outcome was the scenes of rural life in Adam Bede and The Mill on the Floss. Wordsworth, reared amongst the mountains, becomes a very prophet of Nature; while Tennyson draws endless imagery from the levels of the eastern counties where he was brought up. Little David Copperfield was "a very observant child, though," says he, "I think the memory of most of us can go farther back into such times than many of us suppose; just as I believe the power of observation in numbers of very young children to be quite wonderful for its closeness and accuracy. Indeed, I think that most grown men who are remarkable in this respect may with greater propriety be said not to have lost the faculty, than to have! acquired it; the rather, as I generally observe such men to retain a certain freshness, and gentleness, and capacity of being pleased, which are also an inheritance they have preserved from their childhood";—in which remark Dickens makes his hero talk sound philosophy as well as kindly sense.

VIII. THE CHILD SHOULD BE MADE FAMILIAR WITH NATURAL OBJECTS

An Observant Child should be put in the way of Things worth Observing.—But what is the use of being a 'very observant child,' if you are not put in the way of things worth observing? And here is the difference between the streets of a town and the sights and sounds of the country. There is plenty to be seen in a town and children accustomed to the ways of the streets become nimble-witted enough. But the scraps of information to be picked up in a town are isolated fragments; they do not hang on to anything else, nor come to anything more; the information may be convenient, but no one is the wiser for knowing which side of the street is Smith's, and which turning leads to Thompson's shop.

Every Natural Object a Member of a Series.—Now take up a natural object, it does not matter what, and you are studying one of a group, a member of a series; whatever knowledge you get about it is so much towards the science which includes all of its kind. Break off an elder twig in the spring; you notice a ring of wood round a centre of pith, and there you have at a glance a distinguishing character of a great division of the vegetable world. You pick up a pebble. Its edges are perfectly smooth and rounded: why? you ask. It is water-worn, weatherworn. And that little pebble brings you face to face with disintegration, the force to which, more than to any other, we owe the aspects of the world which we call picturesque—glen, ravine, valley, hill. It is not necessary that the child should be told anything about disintegration or dicotyledon, only that he should observe the wood and pith in the hazel twig, the pleasant roundness of! the pebble; by-and-by he will! learn the bearing of the facts with which he is already familiar—a very different thing from learning the reason why of facts which have never come under his notice.

Power will pass, more and more, into the hands of Scientific Men.—It is infinitely well worth of the mother's while to take some pains every day to secure, in the first place, that her children spend hours daily amongst rural and natural objects; and, in the second place, to infuse into them, or rather to cherish in them, the love of investigation. "I say it deliberately," says Kingsley, "as a student of society and of history: power will pass more and more into the hands of scientific men. They will rule, and they will act—cautiously, we may hope, and modestly, and charitably—because in learning true knowledge they will have learnt also their own ignorance, and the vastness, the complexity, the mystery of Nature. But they will also be able to rule, they will be able to act, because they have taken the trouble to learn the facts and the laws of Nature."

Intimacy with Nature makes for Personal Well-being.—But to enable them to swim with the stream is the least of the benefits this early training should confer on the children; a love of Nature, implanted so early that it will seem to them hereafter to have been born in them, will enrich their lives with pure interests, absorbing pursuits, health, and good humour. "I have seen," says the same writer, "the young man of fierce passions and uncontrollable daring expend healthily that energy which threatened daily to plunge him into recklessness, if not into sin, upon hunting out and collecting, through rock and bog, snow and tempest, every bird and egg of the neighbouring forest... I have seen the young London beauty, amid all the excitement and temptation of luxury and flattery, with her heart pure, and her mind occupied in a boudoir full of shells and fossils, flowers and seaweeds, keeping herself unspotted from the world, by considering the lilies of the fields of the field, how they grow."

Volume 3, pages 236 - 238

'Practical Instruction.'—To turn to the question of practical instruction, under the heads of 'Science, Drawing, Manual and Physical Training,' etc., I can do no more here than repeat our convictions. We believe that education under these four heads is due to every child of whatever class; and, for boys and girls under twelve, probably the same general curriculum would be suitable for all. I have nothing to add to the sound ideas as to the teaching of each of these subjects which are now common property.

Science.—In Science, or rather, nature study, we attach great importance to recognition, believing that the power to recognise and name a plant or stone or constellation involves classification and includes a good deal of knowledge. To know a plant by its gesture and habitat, its time and its way of flowering and fruiting; a bird by its flight and song and its times of coming and going; to know when, year after year, you may come upon the redstart and the pied fly-catcher, means a good deal of interested observation, and of; at any rate, the material for science. The children keep a dated record of what they see in their nature note-books, which are left to their own management and are not corrected.

These note-books are a source of pride and joy, and are freely illustrated by drawings (brushwork) of twig, flower, insect, etc. The knowledge necessary for these records is not given in the way of teaching.

On one afternoon in the week, the children (of the Practising School) go for a 'nature walk' with their teachers. They notice for themselves, and the teacher gives a name or other information as it is asked for, and it is surprising what a range of knowledge a child of nine or ten acquires.

The teachers are careful not to make these nature walks an opportunity for scientific instruction, as we wish the children's attention to be given to observation with very little direction. In this way they lay up that store of 'common information' which Huxley considered should precede science teaching; and, what is much more important, they learn to know and delight in natural objects as in the familiar faces of friends. The nature-walk should not be made the occasion to impart a sort of Tit-Bits miscellany of scientific information.

The study of science should be pursued in an ordered sequence, which is not possible or desirable in a walk. It seems to me a sine quâ non of a living education that all school children of whatever grade should have one half-day in the week, throughout the year, in the fields. There are few towns where country of some sort is not accessible, and every child should have the opportunity of watching from week to week, the procession of the seasons.

Geography, geology, the course of the sun, the behaviour of the clouds, weather signs, all that the 'open' has to offer, are made use of in these walks; but all is incidental, easy, and things are noticed as they occur. It is probable that in most *neighbourhoods there are naturalists who would be willing to give their help in the 'nature walks' of a given school.*

We supplement this direct 'nature walk' by occasional object-lessons, as, on the hairs of plants, on diversity of wings, on the sorts of matters taken up in Professor Miall's capital books; but our main dependence is on books as an adjunct to out-of-door work—Mrs. Fisher's, Mrs. Brightwen's, Professor Lloyd Morgan's, Professor Geikie's, Professors Geddes' and Thomson's (the two last for children over fourteen), etc., etc. In the books of these and some other authors the children are put in the position of the original observer of biological and other phenomena.

They learn what to observe, and make discoveries for themselves, original so far as they are concerned. They are put in the right attitude of mind for scientific observations and deductions, and their keen interest is awakened.

We are extremely careful not to burden the verbal memory with scientific nomenclature. Children learn of pollen, antennae, and what not, incidentally, when the thing is present and they require a name for it

The children who are curious about it, and they only, should have the opportunity of seeing with the microscope any minute wonder of structure that has come up in their reading or their walks; but a good lens is a capital and almost an indispensable companion in field work.

I think there is danger in giving too prominent a place to education by Things, enormous as is its value; a certain want of atmosphere is apt to result, and a deplorable absence of a standard of comparison and of the principle of veneration. 'We are the people!' seems to be the note of an education which is not largely sustained on books as well as on things.

CHAPTER 9.
SCIENCE BOOKS

In this chapter I am going to walk you through some of my favourite living book titles on the subject of science and nature study. I also have some tips to help you when you're looking for books, so that, when you see a book, you will have a clearer idea of whether you want it in your collection or not. You might remember seeing some of these ideas before. They are so important that they are here again.

NINE TIPS FOR CHOOSING LIVING BOOKS ABOUT NATURE AND SCIENCE

When you are choosing science books to educate your children:

1. Go for real books that anybody would want to read.
2. Look for the best books on science that you can find.
3. Only go to curriculum books and text books as a last resort.
4. Look for books that are written by people who absolutely love their subjects.
5. Look for books that are beautiful and inspiring.
6. Look for books that you want to read yourself, rather than ones that you think would be 'good' for your child to read.
7. Books that you have already read and love are the best, and they should be at the top of your list.
8. Books which tell the story of a great scientist are important because they inspire the reader. Many a scientist chooses his/her career after reading about another scientist who changed the world for the better.
9. Charlotte Mason said 'One of our presumptuous sins in this connection is that we venture to offer opinions to children (and to older persons) instead of ideas.' Try to choose books which present ideas rather than opinions.

A LIST OF MY FAVOURITE SCIENCE BOOKS.

These books are some of the science books that I have used and loved myself. (Some of them are written from a Christian point of view and I have pointed that out in the description.)

Keeping a Nature Journal by Clare Walker Leslie.

I bought this book in 2000 when it was first released and I have recommended it to many people since then. It's inspiring, easy to use and absolutely beautiful. I like the way the authors use very simple techniques to give you confidence as you start your own nature journal. I like the way you are encouraged to observe and then draw what you see. The emphasis is on the drawing, not in the result.

At the same time, experienced journal-keepers are encouraged to develop and hone their powers of observation as they learn more techniques and enjoy this beautiful book.

This is an ideal book for you to get when working with children as young as 5 and up to the age of 12 and beyond. You will be inspired to start your own nature journal and you will be able to inspire your children to take pride in their own nature journals.

Archimedes and the Door to Science by Jeanne Bendick.

This is an excellent science history story book to inspire you and your children. The book is aimed at children who would be reading their own books (age range 9 – 12 years) and doing written narrations. However, there are a lot of activities in the book and lots to talk about, so you may choose to read this book aloud as one of your family read-alouds.

The Mystery of the Periodic Table by Benjamin D Wilker

This is a fabulous book to give to young teens to learn about the scientists who discovered the elements on the Periodic Table. Remember what Descartes said? – 'Scientific truths are battles won.' Here's where you can read about some battles won, as the scientists who discovered various elements are introduced to the reader, along with information on each element.

Galen and the Gateway to Medicine by Jeanne Bendick

This book tells the story of the father of modern medicine, Galen. The book gives background details of life at the time of Galen and explains how people saw the human body, health and sickness in those days. There are maps, diagrams and illustrations to help the reader get a good understanding. This is quite an inspirational history of science book, and it is suitable for children aged 9 and up.

21 Great Scientists Who Believed the Bible by Ann Lamont.

This book is no longer in print, unfortunately. But I am including it here as it's a book we have enjoyed. You can look out for a second-hand copy when you are visiting second hand book shops and garage sales.

21 Great Scientists is a book suitable for readers aged 12 years to adult. It's a 250-page, well-referenced book, with biographies of great scientists like Kepler, Newton, Linnaeus, Euler, Faraday, Morse, Babbage, Joule, Pasteur, Lister, Fleming and others. The scientists' stories are told along with information about their discoveries and inventions. The book is written from a Creationist viewpoint.

Scientists Who Believe

Another book in a similar vein to the one above.

Longitude by Dava Sobel

The subtitle of this book is "The true story of a lone genius who solved the greatest scientific problem of his time." This lone genius was John Harrison, clock maker. The scientific problem was how to work out longitude. This was important for shipping as many ships were wrecked when the mariners miscalculated their longitude and the ships foundered on rocks. The story is brilliantly written, with liveliness and energy, and it deserves the accolades it has received. It's written for adults but will suit young people aged 13 and upwards.

The Illustrated Longitude by Dava Sobel

This is a very beautiful, but more expensive version of the original paperback book. It's worth the extra cost, in my opinion.

Life and her Children by Arabella Buckley

This book is referred to by Charlotte Mason as a text she used in her school, teaching children of ages 9 – 11. You will see references to this book in Volume 1, page 64, and Volume 6, page 219. You might be able to find an online version of this book.

Madame How and Lady Why by Charles Kingsley

(yes, the guy who wrote The Water Babies) This book is referred to by Charlotte Mason as a text she used in her school, teaching children of ages 10 – 12. You will see references to this book in Volume 1, page 64, and Volume 6, page 219. You might be able to find an online version of Madame How and Lady Why

MEET JEAN-HENRI FABRE

Jean-Henri Fabre was a French entomologist who lived in the nineteenth and early twentieth century. Fabre's method of studying the insects was simple observation. In true Charlotte Mason style, Fabre simple watched the insects and then wrote about (narrated) what he saw. His books are entertaining, gentle, honest, and they are certainly treasures. They are perfect for us wanting to teach our children using Charlotte Mason's philosophies and ideas, as observation, drawing and narration fit perfectly with Fabre's style and books.

If you were to come across any of Jean-Henri Fabre's other books in your second hand book shop while fossicking, snaffle them up quickly. I managed to get 'The Story Book of Birds and Beasts' this way, and we have loved reading that book.

Also, take a moment to visit the Jean-Henri Fabre e-museum. http://www.e-fabre.com/en

The Story Book of Science by Jean-Henri Fabre

(first published 1917) This book is a children's story book about nature. There is a story teller called Uncle Paul who tells his niece and nephews stories about nature in such a way that everything is interesting and exciting. There are eighty short chapters, each one illustrating a fact about nature. Subjects covered are things like volcanoes, earthquakes, ants, spiders, metals, paper. The age of the book shows in the charming, old fashioned style, although the science itself is still very accurate.

This book is a true classic; it's a worthy book to have on your book shelf and it's an invaluable teaching tool. It's suitable for children of about nine through to teen years.

Children of the Summer: Henri Fabre's Insects by Margaret J Anderson.

Here's a charming fiction book, written from the point of view of ten-year-old Paul whose father is Jean-Henri Fabre. Paul helps his father collect information for a book about insects. The book has beautiful illustrations, and it's suitable for children aged nine to twelve. This book is out of print, but you can look out for it in second hand book shops. You might have trouble getting hold of a copy, but you'll find it worth the effort.

Fabre's Book of Insects by Jean-Henri Fabre.

A beautifully written book about insects. Warning: this book doesn't have any pictures or drawings; it's all word pictures. It's suitable for teens and adults.

EXPLORING CREATION

The following books are from the "Exploring Creation" series, which is a creationist Christian series for homeschooled children aged up to 12 or so, using some of the ideas and practices of Charlotte Mason. If this book were to be used as part of a formal curriculum, each book would provide enough information and suggested activities for a year's work in science. The reason for going with one of these books is if you want to look at a subject in depth and in a logical way. Many non-text books won't go into enough depth on a particular subject. These books can supplement other books that you find on the subject.

Exploring Creation With Astronomy by Jeannie Fulbright.

This is an Apologia publication, aimed at Christian homeschoolers, aged 7 – 12, my daughter absolutely loved this book. There is also online backup support with pages to print off and include in your child's notebook.

Exploring Creation With Botany by Jeannie Fulbright.

This is an Apologia publication, aimed at Christian homeschoolers, aged 7 – 12. There is also online backup support with pages to print off and include in your child's notebook.

Exploring Creation With Zoology 1.Flying Creatures by Jeannie Fulbright.

This book explores the dynamics of flight and animal classification, bird anatomy, how to attract various bird species to your yard and identify them. The Apologia Zoology text contains actual experiments on the preferences and habits of the birds your children see.

For High School, Apologia has a series of text books. These books could be considered 'living books' in that they are written by a single person (not a committee) and the author loves his subject and is passionate about it.

NATURE GUIDE BOOKS AND EQUIPMENT

If you are like me, you probably need help from books to learn about plants and animals. Even if you were taken on nature walks when you were small, as I was, you will probably still like to have good field guides to help identify local flora and fauna.

8 TIPS FOR CHOOSING FIELD GUIDES AND EQUIPMENT

1. Look for books with clear photographs and good descriptions.
2. Make sure the book covers the animals, birds and plants in the area you live in.
3. You will need guides for birds, trees, wild flowers and plants, animals, insects and spiders.
4. Don't scrimp on guides; they are a vital part of your science kit.
5. Look at getting a good magnifier or a bug viewer. It will make everything so much more interesting. It will make your walks fun and your study more serious.
6. Consider a pair of binoculars. You can use these for looking at the moon and planets. And you can use them for bird and animal watching.
7. If you have a tripod it will make the binoculars more useful and your viewing more successful.
8. Look out for a bird call CD. We find our bird call CD very useful for helping us identify birds that we only hear from a distance but can't catch sight of.

SUMMARY

In this chapter I've shown you some science books that would be suitable for teaching science and I have also shown you how to find science books for yourself.

I've given you tips on how to choose local field guides to help you in your nature observations.

ASSIGNMENT

This chapter's assignment is …

- Take a nature walk with your children. Remember

sunblock, sunhat, water, jersey, comfortable shoes, magnifier and binoculars. Have things in backpacks and allow the children to carry their own supplies.
- Take your drawing books and try to draw one thing. (Hint: it's easier to draw something that doesn't move. Plants don't move much, birds do.)
- Don't go too far, don't spend too long. This way it stays fun.
- Use your youngest person as a gauge for what is too far and too long. This way it is fun for everyone.
- Sort out your science books and make a list of books you would like to borrow from the library and a list of books you want to buy for your home library
- Read from Charlotte Mason's work. Volume 6, page 110 and Volume 6, page 126.
- For extra reading, you might like to look at Volume 6, beginning on page 218. Charlotte Mason makes many references to the teaching of science and of its place in the curriculum.

SUPPLEMENT

Volume 6, page 110

One of our presumptuous sins in this connection is that we venture to offer opinions to children (and to older persons) instead of ideas. We believe that an opinion expresses thought and therefore embodies an idea. Even if it did so once the very act of crystallization into opinion destroys any vitality it may have had; pace [this is Latin and means 'with all due deference to the person named, but disagreeing'] Ruskin, a crystal is not a living body and does not feed men.

We think to feed children on the dogmas of a church, the theorems of Euclid, mere abstracts of history, and we wonder that their education does not seem to take hold of them.

Let us hear M. Fouillée on this subject, for to him the idea is all in all both in philosophy and education. But there is a function of education upon which M. Fouillée hardly touches, that of the formation of habits, physical, intellectual, moral.

"'Scientific truths,' said Descartes, 'are battles won.' Describe to the young the principal and most heroic of these battles; you will thus interest them in the results of science and you will develop in them a scientific spirit by means of the enthusiasm for the conquest of truth. . . . How interesting Arithmetic and Geometry might be if we gave a short history of their principal theorems, if the child were meant to be present at the labours of a Pythagoras, a Plato, a Euclid, or in modern times, of a Descartes, a Pascal, or a Leibnitz. Great theories instead of being lifeless and anonymous abstractions would become living human truths each with its own history like a statue by Michael Angelo or like a painting by Raphael."

Volume 6, page 126

… In my afternoon's reading I came upon another very apposite [i.e. 'well expressed'] remark in the letters of John Stuart Mill. Let me read it to you:

"What the poor, as well as the rich, require is not to be taught other people's opinions, but to be induced and enabled to think for themselves. It is not physical science that will do this, even if they could learn it much more thoroughly than they are able to do.'

"The young people of this country are not to be regenerated by economic doctrine or economic history or physical science; they can only be elevated by ideas which act upon the imagination and act upon the character and influence the soul, and it is the function of all good teachers to bring those ideas before them."

CHAPTER 10.
ESTABLISHING GOOD HABITS

So far we have covered Charlotte Mason's life, her times, her personality and her philosophy. I have challenged you with some ideas. I have given you some pieces to read from her books. We have talked about living books and narration. We looked at 'Outdoor Education', nature studies and teaching science. In this chapter I want to talk to you about what Charlotte Mason had to say about habits. I will introduce you to what Charlotte Mason had to say about habits, and then I will leave you to consider the ideas and think about how this all applies in your family and homeschooling.

One of Charlotte Mason's main philosophies was the importance of establishing good habits with children. In *Home Education - Training and Educating Children under Nine* (Volume One) by Charlotte Mason, one of the sections is entitled *Habit is Ten Natures* and this expression is repeated often in the text.

I want to unpack this statement to understand what it means, and especially how it applies to us as modern-day mothers.

HABIT IS TEN NATURES

Charlotte Mason was a woman of her time. By that I mean that she was aware of and affected by the thinking of her day and by the great thinkers and educationalists of her time.

But she also thought for herself. In the late nineteenth and early twentieth century it was generally believed that "nature" ruled over "nurture"; that a child was "resentful, or stubborn or reckless because it is born in him". This argument still continues today. In fact, you will often see articles in the newspaper or on the Internet about this very subject.

In Charlotte Mason's lifetime some philosophers thought it best to allow a child to "develop unhindered according to the elements of character and disposition that are in him."

So what's changed? Some philosophers today think the same thing, don't they?

Charlotte Mason had a clear opinion on this idea. She said:

The child must not be left to his Human Nature.—This is precisely what half the parents in the world, and three-fourths of the teachers, are content to do. (Volume 1, page 102)

What did she mean by this? Did she mean that a child must not be left to develop unhindered?

Was she saying that we mustn't support a child in his weaknesses?

That we mustn't make allowances for a child's special needs or abilities?

No, I don't think she was saying this at all.

Charlotte Mason had the greatest respect for children as people. She saw them as whole persons, fully human and fully alive. She loved children and she wasn't interested in subjugating or browbeating them.

She also wasn't interested in idealising children or excusing or pandering to them. She believed that children needed to be loved in a strong, firm way. They needed to be guided and taught, rather than being left to rule unhappily, because children who are given too much power become insecure and miserable.

When Charlotte Mason wrote about habits, she was saying something very profound. And when we parents fully grasp this wisdom it will change the way we parent our children at a fundamental level.

This is what she was saying:

Habits established in children by parents can and do affect the child's life -

- in performance,
- in attitude, and
- in perception.

She believed that habit could be more powerful than "nature" in all these three areas. Hence "habit is ten natures". That is the power we have, as parents when we choose to set in place good habits for ourselves and for our families.

THE CHARACTER OF THE MAN

Charlotte Mason said: *The habits of the child produce the character of the man...'* (Volume 1, page 118)

Now this takes a bit of thinking about. It's a bold statement. Is she right?

Are we sure? Let's consider how this plays out in real life...

To start with, let's consider the three broad categories of habit that Charlotte Mason listed. She talked about physical habits, intellectual habits and moral habits.

Physical Habits

Can you think of any physical habits? What about things like picking up toys or remembering to hang up the towels after a bath. Can you think of other physical habits? Try to think of something in your own home that everyone always does. There will be more than one, you will have your own list, but I am certain that there will be some (good) physical habits you have in place in your home.

Intellectual Habits

Can you think of any intellectual habits that you have in place or would like to have in place in your home? This is anything connected with your home learning. You are sure to have something in place here. Good intellectual habits might be writing every morning, following your timetable, reading aloud to the children after lunch. In a Charlotte Mason environment, there might be the habit of attention, or narration after only one telling, or neat writing.

It's more likely that you have a list of intellectual habits you would like to see in place, but they are not there yet. That's not unusual, so don't feel bad if that's you.

Moral Habits

Can you think of any moral habits that you have in place in your family? You may have cultivated the habit of truthfulness, or courtesy, or controlled temper.

I would like to end with a quotation from Charlotte Mason. This is a fabulous quotation because it's so true and it presents such a challenge. It also gives me great hope for the future in what I can achieve in and with my family in the formation of habits. Here it is, from Volume 1, page 105:

A mother forms her children's habits involuntarily ... and as a matter of fact, there is nothing which a mother cannot bring her child up to, and there is hardly a mother anywhere who has not some two or three ... principles which her children never violate.

SUMMARY

In this chapter I have talked about habits. We have seen how Charlotte Mason saw habits as being so important that she said 'habit is ten natures' and that habits produce the character of the man.

We've looked at three broad categories of habit and how they apply to everyday life for homeschoolers.

ASSIGNMENT

For this chapter I have picked out some of Charlotte Mason's writings for you to read. And the subject is.... Surprise! ... Habit.

In Volume One, "Home Education" there are two big sections about habit. The first one goes from page 96 to page 135. If you could read the whole section you would do brilliantly.

If you are short of time you could read what I have included as this chapter's supplement, which is: Pages 121 – 132

SUPPLEMENT

This supplement contains your minimum reading. You might want to get out your own copy of Charlotte Mason's Original Homeschool Series to read more.

VOLUME 1, PAGE 121 - 132

Habit a Delight in itself.—*...the forming of habits in the children is no laborious task, for the reward goes hand in hand with the labour; so much so, that it is like the laying out of a penny with the certainty of the immediate return of a pound. For a habit is a delight in itself; poor human nature is conscious of the ease that it is to repeat the doing of anything without effort; and, therefore, the formation of a habit, the gradually lessening sense of effort in a given act, is pleasurable.*

This is one of the rocks that mothers sometimes split upon: they lose sight of the fact that a habit, even a good habit, becomes a real pleasure; and when the child has really formed the habit of doing a certain thing, his mother imagines that the effort is as great to him as at first, that it is virtue in him to go on making this effort, and that he deserves, by way of reward, a little relaxation—she will let him break through the new habit a few times, and then go on again.

But it is not going on; it is beginning again, and beginning in the face of obstacles. The 'little relaxation' she allowed her child meant the forming of another contrary habit, which must be overcome before the child gets back to where he was before.

As a matter of fact, this misguided sympathy on the part of mothers is the one thing that makes it a laborious undertaking to train a child in good habits; for it is the nature of the child to take to habits as kindly as the infant takes to his mother's milk.

Tact, Watchfulness, and Persistence.—*For example, and to choose a habit of no great consequence except as a matter of consideration for others: the mother wishes her child to acquire the habit of shutting the door after him when he enters or leaves a room. Tact, watchfulness, and persistence are the qualities she must cultivate in herself; and, with these, she will be astonished at the readiness with which the child picks up the new habit.*

Stages in the Formation of a Habit.—*'Johnny,' she says, in a bright, friendly voice, 'I want you to remember something with* all your might: never go into or out of a room in which anybody is sitting without shutting the door.'

'But if I forget, mother?'

'I will try to remind you.'

'But perhaps I shall be in a great hurry.'

'You must always make time to do that.'

'But why, mother?'

'Because it is not polite to the people in the room to make them uncomfortable.'

'But if I am going out again that very minute?'

'Still, shut the door, when you come in; you can open it again to go out. Do you think you can remember?'

'I'll try, mother.'

'Very well; I shall watch to see how few "forgets" you make.'

For two or three times Johnny remembers; and then, he is off like a shot and half-way downstairs before his mother has time to call him back.

She does not cry out, 'Johnny, come back and shut the door!' because she knows that a summons of that kind is exasperating to big or little.

She goes to the door, and calls pleasantly, 'Johnny!'

Johnny has forgotten all about the door; he wonders what his mother wants, and, stirred by curiosity, comes back, to find her seated and employed as before.

She looks up, glances at the door, and says, 'I said I should try to remind you.'

'Oh, I forgot,' says Johnny, put upon his honour; and he shuts the door that time, and the next, and the next.

But the little fellow has really not much power to recollect, and the mother will have to adopt various little devices to remind him; but of two things she will be careful—that he never slips off without shutting the door, and that she never lets the matter be a cause of friction between herself and the child, taking the line of his friendly ally to help him against that bad memory of his. By and by, after, say, twenty shuttings of the door with never an omission, the habit begins to be formed; Johnny shuts the door as a matter of course, and his mother watches him with delight come into a room, shut the door, take something off the table, and go out, again shutting the door.

The Dangerous Stage.—Now that Johnny always shuts the

door, his mother's joy and triumph begin to be mixed with unreasonable pity.

'Poor child,' she says to herself, 'it is very good of him to take so much pains about a little thing, just because he is bid!' She thinks that, all the time, the child is making an effort for her sake; losing sight of the fact that the habit has become easy and natural, that, in fact, Johnny shuts the door without knowing that he does so.

Now comes the critical moment. Some day Johnny is so taken up with a new delight that the habit, not yet fully formed, loses its hold, and he is half-way downstairs before he thinks of the door. Then he does think of it, with a little prick of conscience, strong enough, not to send him back, but to make him pause a moment to see if his mother will call him back.

She has noticed the omission, and is saying to herself, 'Poor little fellow, he has been very good about it this long time; I'll let him off this once.' He, outside, fails to hear his mother's call, says, to himself—fatal sentence!—'Oh, it doesn't matter,' and trots off.

Next time he leaves the door open, but it is not a 'forget.' His mother calls him back in a rather feeble way. His quick ear catches the weakness of her tone, and, without coming back, he cries, 'Oh, mother, I'm in such a hurry,' and she says no more, but lets him off. Again he rushes in, leaving the door wide open.

'Johnny! -in a warning voice.

'I'm going out again just in a minute, mother,' and after ten minutes' rummaging he does go out, and forgets to shut the door.

The mother's mis-timed easiness has lost for her every foot of the ground she had gained.

VIII.—INFANT 'HABITS'

The whole group of habitudes, half physical and half moral, on which the propriety and comfort of everyday life depend, are received passively by the child; that is, he does very little to form these habits himself, but his brain receives impressions from what he sees about him; and these impressions take form as his own very strongest and most lasting habits.

Some Branches of Infant Education.—Cleanliness, order, neatness, regularity, punctuality, are all 'branches' of infant education. They should be about the child like the air he breathes, and he will take them in as unconsciously. It is hardly necessary to say a word about the necessity for delicate cleanliness in the nursery.

The babies get their share of tubbing, and unlimited washing is done on their behalf; but, indeed, scrupulous as mothers of the cultured class are, a great deal rests with the nurses, and it needs much watchfulness to secure that there shall not be the faintest odour about the infant or anything belonging to him, and that the nurseries be kept sweet and thoroughly aired.

One great difficulty is, that there are still some nurses who belong to a class to which an open window is an abomination; and another is, they do not all know the meaning of odours: they cannot see 'a smell,' and, therefore, it is not easy to persuade them that a smell is matter, microscopic particles which the child takes into him with every breath he draws.

A Sensitive Nose.—By the way, a very important bit of physical education for a child is to train in him a sensitive nose—nostrils which sniff out the least 'stuffiness' in a room, or the faintest odour attached to clothes or furniture.

The sense of smell appears to have been given us not only as an avenue of pleasure, but as a sort of danger-signal to warn us of the presence of noxious matters: yet many people appear to go through the world without a nose at all; and the fact tends to show that a quick sense of smell is a matter of education and habit.

The habit is easily formed. Encourage the children to notice whether the room they enter 'smells' quite fresh when they come in out of the open air, to observe the difference between the air of the town and the fresher air beyond; and train them to perceive the faintest trace of pleasant or harmless odours.

The Baby is Ubiquitous.—To return to the nursery. It would be a great thing if the nurse could be impressed with the notion that the baby is ubiquitous, and that he not only sees and knows everything, but will keep, for all his life, the mark of all he sees.—

"If there's a hole in a' your coats,
I pray ye, tent it;
A chiel's amang ye takin' notes,
And, faith, he'll prent it": -
'prent it' on his own active brain, as a type for his future habits.

Such a notion on the nurse's part might do something to secure cleanliness that goes beyond that of clean aprons. One or two little bits of tidiness that nurses affect are not to be commended on the score of cleanliness—the making up of the nursery beds early in the morning, and the folding up of the children's garments when they take them off at night. It is well to stretch a line across the day nursery at night, and hang the little garments out for an airing, to get rid of the insensible perspiration with which they have been laden during the day. For the same reason, the beds and bedclothes should be turned down to air for a couple of hours before they are made up.

Personal Cleanliness as an Early Habit.—The nursery table, if there be one, should be kept as scrupulously nice as that of the dining-room. The child who sits down to a crumpled or spotted tablecloth, or uses a discoloured metal spoon, is degraded—by so much.

The children, too, should be encouraged to nice cleanliness in their own persons. We have all seen the dainty baby-hand stretched out to be washed; it has got a smudge, and the child does not like it. May they be as particular when they are big enough to wash their own hands!

Not that they should be always clean and presentable; children love to 'mess about' and should have big pinafores for the purpose. They are all like that little French prince who scorned his birthday gifts, and entreated to be allowed to make dear little mud-pies with the boy in the gutter.

Let them make their mud-pies freely; but that over, they should be impatient to remove every trace of soil, and should do it themselves. Young children may be taught to take care of their fingernails, and to cleanse the corners of eyes and ears.

As for sitting down to table with unwashed hands and unbrushed hair, that, of course, no decent child is allowed to do.

Children should be early provided with their own washing materials, and accustomed to find real pleasure in the bath, and in attending to themselves.

There is no reason why a child of five or six should not make himself thoroughly clean without all that torture of soap in the eyes and general pulling about and poking which children hate, and no wonder. Besides, the child is not getting the habit of the daily bath until he can take it for himself, and it is important that this habit should be formed before the reckless era of school-life begins.

Modesty and Purity.—The operations of the bath afford the mother opportunities to give necessary teaching and training in habits of decency, and a sense of modesty. To let her young child live and grow in Eden-like simplicity is, perhaps, the most tempting and natural course to the mother. But alas! we do not live in the Garden, and it may be well that the child should be trained from the first to the conditions under which he is to live. To the youngest child, as to our first parents, there is that which is forbidden.

In the age of unquestioning obedience, let him know that not all of his body does Almighty God allow him to speak of, think of, display, handle, except for purposes of cleanliness. This will be the easier to the mother if she speak of heart, lungs, etc., which, also, we are not allowed to look at or handle, but which have been so enclosed in walls of flesh and bone that we cannot get at them.

That which is left open to us is so left, like that tree in the Garden of Eden, as a test of obedience; and in the one case, as in the other, disobedience is attended with certain loss and ruin.

The Habit of Obedience and the Sense of Honour.—The sense of prohibition, of sin in disobedience, will be a wonderful safeguard against knowledge of evil to the child brought up in habits of obedience; and still more effective will be the sense of honour, of a charge to keep—the motive of the apostolic injunctions on this subject.

Let the mother renew this charge with earnestness on the eve, say, of each birthday, giving the child to feel that by obedience in this matter he may glorify God with his body; let her keep watch against every approach of evil; and let her pray daily that each one of her children may be kept in purity for that day. To ignore the possibilities of evil in this kind is to expose the child to frightful risks.

At the same time, be it remembered that words which were meant to hinder may themselves be the cause of evil, and that a life full of healthy interests and activities is amongst the surest preventives of secret vice.

Order Essential.—What has been said about cleanliness applies as much to order—order in the nursery, and orderly habits in the nurse. One thing under this head: the nursery should not be made the hospital for the disabled or worn-out furniture of the house; cracked cups, chipped plates, jugs and teapots with fractured spouts, should be banished.

The children should be brought up to think that when once an article is made unsightly by soil or fracture it is spoiled, and must be replaced; and this rule will prove really economical, for when children and servants find that things no longer 'do,' after some careless injury, they learn to be careful. But, in any case, it is a real detriment to the children to grow up using imperfect and unsightly makeshifts.

The pleasure grown-up people take in waiting on children is really a fruitful source of mischief;—for instance, in this matter of orderly habits. Who does not know the litter the children leave to be cleared up after them a dozen times a day, in the nursery, garden, drawing-room, wherever their restless little feet carry them? We are a bit sentimental about scattered toys and faded nosegays, and all the tokens of the children's presence; but the fact is, that the lawless habit of scattering should not be allowed to grow upon children.

Everybody condemns the mother of a family whose drawers are chaotic, whose possessions are flung about heedlessly; but at least some of the blame should be carried back to her mother. It is not as a woman that she has picked up a miserable habit which destroys the comfort, if not the happiness, of her home; the habit of disorder was allowed to grow upon her as a child, and her share of the blame is, that she has failed to cure herself.

The Child of Two should put away his Playthings.—The child of two should be taught to get and to replace his playthings.

Begin early. Let it be a pleasure to him, part of his play, to open his cupboard, and put back the doll or the horse each in its own place. Let him always put away his things as a matter of course, and it is surprising how soon a habit of order is formed, which will make it pleasant to the child to put away his toys, and irritating to him to see things in the wrong place.

If parents would only see the morality of order, that order in the nursery becomes scrupulousness in after life, and that the training necessary to form the habit is no more, comparatively, than the occasional winding of a clock, which ticks away then of its own accord and without trouble to itself, more pains would be taken to cultivate this important habit.

Neatness Akin to Order.—Neatness is akin to order, but is not quite the same thing: it implies not only 'a place for everything, and everything in its place,' but everything in a suitable place, so as to produce a good effect; in fact, taste comes into play.

The little girl must not only put her flowers in water. but arrange them prettily, and must not be put off with some rude kitchen mug or jug for them, or some hideous pink vase, but must have jar or vase graceful in form and harmonious in hue, though it be but a cheap trifle. In the same way, everything in the nursery should be 'neat'—that is, pleasing and suitable; and children should be encouraged to make neat and effective arrangements of their own little properties.

Nothing vulgar in the way of print, picture-book, or toy should be admitted—nothing to vitiate a child's taste or introduce a strain of commonness into his nature. On the other hand, it would be hard to estimate the refining, elevating influence of one or two well-chosen works of art, in however cheap a reproduction.

Regularity.—The importance of Regularity in infant education is beginning to be pretty generally acknowledged. The young mother knows that she must put her baby to bed at a proper time, regardless of his cries, even if she leave him to cry two or three times, in order that, for the rest of his baby life, he may put himself sweetly to sleep in the dark without protest.

But a good deal of nonsense is talked about the reason of the child's cries—he is supposed to want his mother, or his nurse, or his bottle, or the light, and to be 'a knowing little fellow,' according to his nurse, quite up to the fact that if he cries for these things he will get them.

Habits of Time and Place.—The fact is, the child has already formed a habit of wakefulness or of feeding at improper times, and he is as uneasy at his habits being broken in upon as the cat is at a change of habitation; when he submits happily to the new regulation, it is because the new habit is formed, and is, in its turn, the source of satisfaction.

According to Dr Carpenter, "Regularity should begin even with infant life, as to times of feeding, repose, etc. The bodily habit thus formed greatly helps to shape the mental habit at a later period.

On the other hand, nothing tends more to generate a habit of self-indulgence than to feed a child, or to allow it to remain out of bed, at unseasonable times, merely because it cries. It is wonderful how soon the actions of a young infant (like those of a young dog or horse) come into harmony with systematic 'training' judiciously exercised"

The habit of regularity is as attractive to older children as to the infant. The days when the usual programme falls through are, we know, the days when the children are apt to be naughty.

CHAPTER 11.
HABITS – A CLOSER LOOK

Let's continue to look more closely at the subject of habits. We will look at specific habits and consider which habits Charlotte Mason regarded as worth working on. As you read, you will see that I am recommending particular pages from *Home Education* and these page are included in this chapter's supplement.

HABITS

I love the way Charlotte Mason says: *Education in habit favours an easy life.* (page 135 of Volume 1).

Isn't this a great thought?

It really is a great thought, and not just an interesting idea. If you can get hold of this message you will have strong motivation to instil good habits in your life and the life of your child.

Charlotte Mason says it is because *it is pleasant to know that, even in mature life, it is possible by a little persistent effort to acquire a desirable habit.*

So how do you acquire good habits?

THE FORMATION OF A HABIT

This was part of your assignment reading last chapter. Did you like the way Charlotte Mason gives us very clear steps on the formation of a habit?

I don't know about you, but my own experience is as Charlotte Mason describes. Especially when she talks about the dangerous stage in habit formation.

It's so true, isn't it?

And I think that knowing that the dangerous stage is there is a great help in avoiding failure in habit formation.

SOME HABITS TO CONSIDER AND READ ABOUT

Let's look at some particular habits that Charlotte Mason discusses now. For the rest of this chapter I will be referring to some pages from Charlotte Mason's *Volume One Home Education*. You will find these pages in your supplement.

Charlotte Mason saw some habits as being inspired by the atmosphere of the home, and some that required direct teaching.

Attention. This habit is discussed in detail in Volume One, starting at page 137, and it's certainly worth reading. Charlotte Mason spoke very strongly and eloquently of the habit of attention, which was of immense importance to her. She said:

It is impossible to overstate the importance of this habit of attention. It is, to quote the words of weight, 'within the reach of every one, and should be made the primary object of all mental discipline'; for whatever the natural gifts of the child, it is only in so far as the habit of attention is cultivated in him that he is able to make use of them. (page 146)

This is a strong statement: 'impossible to overstate the importance of this habit'. And the child is only able to make use of whatever natural gifts he has 'in so far as the habit of attention is cultivated in him'.

I have a few questions for you to think about:

- Do you agree with Charlotte Mason?
- Can you see why she thought it was so important?
- Will you be cultivating this habit in your family?

Application. Just think about this, the habit of application to a job in hand. Had you thought of this as being a habit? (you can read about this on page 149)

Thinking. The habit of thinking? Did you ever consider that thinking was a habit? What did Charlotte Mason mean? She explains all on pages 150 and 151. And I would like to add my own opinion that I think that it's also the habit of thinking right thoughts. Of being in charge of thoughts, rather than thoughts ruling the person.

Imagining. The habit of imagining. Charlotte Mason's words on this are on page 151 – 154. I like what she says. And I also think, myself, that it's a lack of imagination for adults which causes many problems. If you can imagine what another person feels like you will act more wisely. If you can imagine how good something will be when a task is completed you will be motivated to complete the task. And so on...

Remembering. Read page 154 to 159.

Perfect execution. This starts on page 159.

Obedience. This is a moral habit, and one we definitely want our children to acquire. It's very difficult to homeschool effectively if your child is disobedient. Start reading on page 160. I really like that Charlotte Mason talks about children having the 'desire to obey'. (What bliss that would be!)

Truthfulness. Charlotte Mason's notes start on page 164. She talks about the importance of truthfulness and discusses the three causes of lying.

Sweet temper. Ah.... This is so cool! The *habit* of sweet temper? If you have ever been confronted by a child who is feisty or aggressive, (or maybe you battle feistiness in yourself) you will be extremely interested in this darling habit. Sweet temper is a habit? Yes, for some, it is a habit. There are those who are blessed with the tendency to sweet nature. Others have to work at it, but can achieve the habit of sweet temper.

This idea of habits, and of training children in the way they should go, is one that develops and grows and becomes clearer the more you consider it.

And also, sooner or later, you come to the realisation that not only does the parent need to train the child in good habits, but the parent has some self-training in habits to do.

Sheeesh!

It's ourselves we need to train!

... er ... I think we should move on now....

PARENTS AS INSPIRERS

Charlotte Mason made a point of clarifying the role of parents as *inspirer* instead of *shaper*. By this she meant that we are not to attempt to shape or form our children, as though they are clay. Instead we are to inspire our children.

This, again, puts the onus on the parent. It's our own behaviour that we need to address first. We need to have good habits in place and to be an inspiration to our children.

This doesn't mean that we don't actively parent our children.

And, in fact, Charlotte Mason gives many examples of exactly how to teach and guide the children. But we do it with a certain confident and inspiring attitude. As we grow and develop our own good habits, we also guide our children and instil good habits in our families.

SUMMARY

In this chapter

- I have talked about how a good habit is actually formed, various desirable habits, and in particular, the habit of attention.
- We've looked at our own role in developing good habits in the family – how we need to lead by example, and see ourselves as inspirers, rather than creators. And we've considered the implications to ourselves and our families of developing good habits in our families.

ASSIGNMENT

Read the pages in the Supplement and then consider these questions.

Questions:

- How do you establish habits in your home?
- What have you had success with?
- Which habit would you like to train your children in next?
- Have you seen habits established in other families? How did they do it, and how can we learn from each other?
- What do you think are age-appropriate habits?

Reading:

- Volume 1, pages 145 – 168
- Volume 5. Try a couple of stories from part one. You could try chapter 1, 'The Philosopher at Home' and chapter 2, 'Inconstant Kitty'.

SUPPLEMENT

For your supplement this chapter I have included pages 137 – 168 of *Home Education* on the subject of Habits. I have included the page numbers so that you can find your way easily through the pages and refer to the notes in the lesson.

Volume 1, page 137 - 168
I. The Habit of Attention

Let us pass on, now, to the consideration of a group of mental habits which are affected by direct training rather than by example.

First, we put the habit of Attention, because the highest intellectual gifts depend for their value upon the measure in which their owner has cultivated the habit of attention. To explain why this habit is of such supreme importance, we must consider the operation of one or two of the laws of thought. But just recall, in the meantime, the fixity of attention with which the trained professional man—the lawyer, the doctor, the man of letters—listens to a roundabout story, throws out the padding, seizes the facts, sees the bearing of every circumstance, and puts the case with new clearness and method; and contrast this with the wandering eye and random replies of the uneducated;—and you see that to differentiate people according to their power of attention is to employ a legitimate test.

[page 138]

A Mind at the Mercy of Associations.*—We will consider, then, the nature and the functions of attention. The mind—with the possible exception of the state of coma—is never idle; ideas are for ever passing through the brain, by day and by night, sleeping or walking, mad or sane. We take a great deal too much upon ourselves when we suppose that we are the authors and intenders of the thoughts we think. The most we can do is to give direction to these trains of thought in the comparatively few moments when we are regulating the thoughts of our hearts. We see in dreams—the rapid dance of ideas through the brain during lighter sleep—how ideas follow one another in a general way. In the wanderings of delirium, in the fancies of the mad, the inconsequent prattle of the child, and the babble of the old* man, we see the same thing, i.e.—the law according to which ideas course through the mind when they are left to themselves. You talk to a child about glass—you wish to provoke a proper curiosity as to how glass is made, and what are its uses. Not a bit of it; he wanders off to Cinderella's glass slipper; then he tells you about his godmother who gave him a boat; then about the ship in which Uncle Harry went to America; then he wonders why you do not wear spectacles, leaving you to guess that Uncle Harry does so. But the child's ramblings are not whimsical; they follow a law, the law of association of ideas, by which any idea presented to the mind recalls some other idea which has been at any time associated with it—as glass and Cinderella's slipper; and that, again some idea associated with it. Now this law of association of ideas is a good servant and a bad mater. To have this aid in recalling the events of the past, the engagements

[page 139]

of the present, is an infinite boon; but to be at the mercy of associations, to have no power to think what we choose when we choose, but only as something 'puts it into our head,' is to be no better than an imbecile.

Wandering Attention.—A vigorous effort of will should enable us at any time to fix our thoughts. Yes; but a vigorous self-compelling will is the flower of a developed character; and while the child has no character to speak of, but only natural disposition, who is to keep humming-tops out of a geography lesson, or a doll's sofa out of a French verb? Here is the secret of the weariness of the home schoolroom—the children are thinking all the time about something else than their lessons; or rather, they are at the mercy of the thousand fancies that flit through their brains, each in the train of the last. "Oh, Miss Smith," said a little girl to her governess, "there are so many things more interesting than lessons to think about!"

Where is the harm? In this: not merely that the children are wasting time, though that is a pity; but that they are forming a desultory habit of mind and reducing their own capacity for mental effort.

The Habit of Attention to be Cultivated in the Infant.— The help, then, is not the will of the child but in the habit of attention, a habit to be cultivated even in the infant. A baby, notwithstanding his wonderful powers of observation, has no power of attention; in a minute, the covered plaything drops from listless little fingers, and the wandering glance lights upon some new joy. But even at this stage the habit of attention may be trained: the discarded plaything is picked up, and, with 'Pretty!' and dumb

[page 140]

show, the mother keeps the infant's eyes fixed for fully a couple of minutes—and this is her first lesson in attention. Later, as we have seen, the child is eager to see and handle every object that comes in his way. But watch him at his investigations: he flits from thing to thing with less purpose than a butterfly amongst the flowers, staying at nothing long enough to get the good out of it. It is the mother's part to supplement the child's quick observing faculty with the habit of attention. She must see to it that he does not flit from this to that but looks long enough at one thing to get a real acquaintance with it.

Is little Margaret fixing round eyes on a daisy she has plucked? In a second, the daisy will be thrown away, and a pebble or buttercup will charm the little maid. But the mother seizes the happy moment. She makes Margaret see that the daisy is a bright yellow eye with white eyelashes round it; that all the day long it lies there in the grass and looks up at the great sun, never blinking as Margaret would do, but keeping its eyes wide open. And that is why it is called daisy, 'day's eye,' because its eye is always looking at the sun which makes the day. And what does Margaret think it does at night, when there is no sun? It does what little boys and girls do; it just shuts up its eye with its white lashes tipped with pink, and goes to sleep till the sun comes again in the morning. By this time the daisy has become interesting to Margaret; she looks at it with big eyes after her mother has finished speaking, and then, very likely, cuddles it up to her breast or gives it a soft little kiss. Thus the mother will contrive ways to invest every object in the child's world with interest and delight.

[page 141]

Attention to 'Things'; Words at Weariness.—But the tug of war begins with the lessons of the schoolroom. Even the child who has gained the habit of attention to things, finds words a weariness. This is a turning point in the child's life, and the moment for mother's tact and vigilance. In the first place, never let the child dawdle over copybook or sum, sit dreaming with his book before him. When a child grows stupid over a lesson, it is time to put it away. Let him do another lesson as unlike the last as possible, and then go back with freshened wits to his unfinished task. If mother or governess have been unwary enough to let the child 'moon' over a lesson, she must just exert her wits to pull him through; the lesson must be done, of course, but must be made bright and pleasant to the child.

Lessons Attractive.—The teacher should have some knowledge of the principles of education; should know what subjects are best fitted for the child considering his age, and how to make these subjects attractive; should know, too, how to vary the lessons, so that each power of the child's mind should rest after effort, and some other power be called into play. She should know how to incite the child to effort through his desire of approbation, of excelling, of advancing, his desire of knowledge, his love of his parents, his sense of duty, in such a way that no one set of motives be called unduly into play to the injury of the child's character. But the danger she must be especially alive to, is the substitution of any other natural desire for that of knowledge, which is equally natural, and is adequate for all the purposes of education.

[page 142]

Time-table; Definite Work in a Given Time.—I shall have opportunities to enter into some of these points later; meantime, let us look in at a home schoolroom managed on sound principles. In the first place, there is a time-table, written out fairly, so that the child knows what he has to do and how long each lesson is to last. This idea of definite work to be finished in a given time is valuable to the child, not only as training him in habits of order, but in diligence; he learns that one time is not 'as good as another'; that there is no right time left for what is not done in its own time; and this knowledge alone does a great deal to secure the child's attention to his work. Again, the lessons are short, seldom more than twenty minutes in length for children under eight; and this, for two or three reasons. The sense that there is not much time for his sums or his reading, keeps the child's wits on the alert and helps to fix his attention; he has time to learn just so much of any one subject as it is good for him to take in at once: and if the lessons be judiciously alternated—sums first, say, while the brain is quite fresh; then writing, or reading—some more or less mechanical exercise, by way of a rest; and so on, the program varying a little from day to day, but the same principle throughout—a 'thinking' lesson first, and a 'painstaking' lesson to follow,—the child gets through his morning lessons without any sign of weariness.

Even with regular lessons and short lessons, a further stimulus may be occasionally necessary to secure the attention of the child. His desire of approbation may ask the stimulus, not only of a word of praise, Btu of something in the shape of a reward to secure his utmost efforts. Now, rewards should be dealt

[page 143]

out to the child upon principle: they should be the natural consequences of his good conduct.

A Natural Reward.—What is the natural consequence of work well and quickly done? Is it not the enjoyment of ampler leisure? The boy is expected to do two right sums in twenty minutes: he does them in ten minutes; the remaining ten minutes are his own, fairly earned, in which he should be free for a scamper in the garden, or any delight he chooses. His writing task is to produce six perfect m's: he writes six lines with only one good m in each line, the time for the writing lesson is over and he has none for himself; or, he is able to point out six good m's in his first line, and he has the rest of the time to draw steamboats and railway trains. This possibility of letting the children occupy themselves variously in the few minutes they may gain at the end of each lesson, is compensation which the home schoolroom offers for the zest which the sympathy of numbers, and emulation, are supposed to give to schoolwork.

Emulation.—As for emulation, a very potent means of exciting and holding the attention of children, it is often objected that a desire to excel, to do better than others, implies an unloving temper, which the educator should rather repress than cultivate. Good marks of some kind are usually the rewards of those who do best, and it is urged that these good marks are often the cause of ungenerous rivalry. Now, the fact is, the children are being trained to live in the world, and in the world we all do get good marks of one kind or another, prize, or praise, or both, according as we excel others, whether in football or tennis, or in picture painting or poem-making.

[page 144]

There are envyings and heart burnings amongst those who

come in second best; so it has been from beginning, and doubtless will be to the end. If the child is go out into an emulous world, why, it may be possibly be well that he should brought up in an emulous school. But here is where the mother's work comes in. She can teach her child to be first without vanity, and to be last without bitterness; that is, she can bring him up in such a hearty outgoing of love and sympathy that joy in his brother's success takes the sting out of his own failure, and regret for his brother's failure leaves no room for self-glorification. Again, if a system of marks be used as a stimulus to attention and effort, the good marks should be given for conduct rather than for cleverness—that is, they should be within everybody's reach: every child may get his mark for punctuality, order, attention, diligence, obedience, gentleness; and therefore, marks of this kind may be given without danger of leaving a rankling sense of injustice in the breast of the child who fails. Emulation becomes suicidal when it is used as the incentive to intellectual effort, because the desire for knowledge subsides in proportion as the desire to excel becomes active. As a matter of fact, marks of any sort, even for conduct, distract the attention of children from their proper work, which is in itself interesting enough to secure good behaviour as well as attention.

Affection as a Motive.—That he ought to work hard to please his parents who do so much for him, is a proper motive to bring before the child from time to time, but not too often: if the mother trade on her child's feelings, if, 'Do this or that to please mother,' 'Do not grieve poor mother,' etc., be brought too frequently

[page 145]

before the child as the reason for right doing, a sentimental relation is set up which both parent and child will find embarrassing, the true motives of action will be obscured, and the child unwilling to appear unloving, will end in being untrue.

Attractiveness of Knowledge.—Of coups, the most obvious means of quickening and holding the attention of children lies in the attractiveness of knowledge itself, and in the real appetite for knowledge with which they are endowed. But how successful faulty teachers are in curing children of any desire to know, is to be seen in many a school room. I shall later, however, have an opportunity for a few words on this subject.

What is Attention?—It is evident that attention is no 'faculty' of the mind; indeed, it is very doubtful how far the various operations of the mind should be described as 'faculties' at all. Attention is hardly even an operation of the mind, but is simply the act by which the whole mental force is applied to the subject in hand. This act, of bringing the whole mind to bear, may be trained into a habit at the will of the parent or teacher, who attracts and holds the child's attention by means of a sufficient motive

Self-Compelled.—As the child gets older, he is taught to bring his own will to bear; to make himself attend in spite of the most inviting suggestions from without. He should be taught to feel a certain triumph in compelling himself to fix his thoughts. Let him know what the real difficulty is, how it is the nature of his mind to be incessantly thinking, but how the thoughts, if left to themselves, will always run off from one thing to another, and that the struggle and the victory required of him is to fix his thoughts upon

[page 146]

the task in hand. 'You have done your duty,' with a look of sympathy from his mother, is a reward for the child who has made this effort in the strength of his growing will. But it cannot be too much borne in mind that attention is, to a great extent, the product of the educated mind; that is, one can only attend in proportion as one has the intellectual power of developing the topic.

It is impossible to overstate the importance of this habit of attention. It is, to quote words of weight, "within the reach of everyone, and should be made the primary object of all mental discipline"; for whatever the natural gifts of the child, it is only so far as the habit of attention is cultivated in him that he is able to make use of them.

The Secret of Overpressure.—If it were only as it saves wear and tear, a perpetual tussle between duty and inclination, it is worthwhile for the mother to lay herself out to secure that her child never does a lesson into which he does not put his heart. And that is no difficult undertaking; the thing is, to be on the watch from the beginning against the formation of the contrary habit of inattention. A great deal has been said lately about overpressure, and we have glanced at one or two of the causes whose effects go by this name. But truly, one of the most fertile causes of an overdone brain is a failure in the habit of attention. I suppose we are all ready to admit that it is not the things we do, but the things we fail to do, which fatigue us, with the sense of omission, with the worry of hurry in overtaking our tasks. And this is almost the only cause of failure in the work in the case of the healthy schoolboy or schoolgirl: wandering wits hinder a lesson from being fully taken in at the right

[page 147]

moment; that lesson becomes a bugbear, continually wanted henceforth and never there; and the sense of loss tries the young scholar more than would the attentive reception of a dozen such lessons.

The Schoolboy's Home Work.—In the matter of homework, the parents may still be of great use to their boys and girls after they begin to go to day-school; not in helping them, that should not be necessary; but let us suppose a case: 'Poor Annie does not her finish her lessons till half past nine, she really has so much to do'; 'Poor Tom is at his books till ten o'clock; we never see anything of the children in the evening,' say the distressed parents; and they let their children go on in a course which is absolutely ruinous both to bodily health and brain power.

Wholesome Home Treatment for Mooning.—Now, the fault is very seldom in the lessons, but in the children; they moon over their books, and a little wholesome home treatment should cure them of that ailment. Allow them, at the utmost, an hour and a half for their home-work; treat them tacitly as defaulters if they do not appear at the end of that time; do not be betrayed into word or look of sympathy; and the moment the time for lessons is over, let some delightful game or storybook be begun in the drawing room. By-and-by they will find that it is possible to finish lessons in time to secure a pleasant evening afterwards, and the lessons will be much the better done for the fact that concentrated attention has been bestowed upon them. At the same time the custom of giving home-work, at any rate to children under fourteen, is greatly to be deprecated. The gain of a combination of home and school life is lost to the

[page 148]

children; and a very full scheme of school work may be carried through in the morning hours.

Rewards and Punishments should be relative Consequences

of Conduct.—In considering the means of securing attention, it has been necessary to refer to discipline—the dealing out of rewards and punishments,—a subject which every tyro of a nursery maid or nursery governess feels herself very competent to handle. But this, too, has its scientific aspect: there is a law by which all rewards and punishments should be regulated: they should be natural, or, at any rate, the relative consequences of conduct; should imitate, as nearly as may be without injury to the child, the treatment which such and such conduct deserves and receives in after life. Miss Edgeworth, in her story of Rosamond and the Purple Jar, hits the right principle, though the incident is rather extravagant. Little girls do not often pine for purple jars in chemists' windows; but that we should suffer for our wilfulness in getting what is unnecessary by going without what is necessary, is precisely one of the lessons of life we all have to learn, and therefore is the right sort of lesson to teach a child.

Natural and Elective Consequences.—It is evident that to administer rewards and punishments on this principle requires patient consideration and steady determination on the mother's part. She must consider with herself what fault of disposition the child's misbehaviour springs from; she must aim her punishment at that fault, and must brace herself to see her child suffer present loss for his lasting gain. Indeed, exceedingly little actual punishment is necessary where children are brought up with care. But this happens continually—the child who has done

[page 149]

well gains some natural reward (like that ten minutes in the garden), which the child forfeits who has done less well; and the mother must brace herself and her child to bear this loss; if she equalise the two children she commits a serious wrong, not against the child who has done well, but against the defaulter, whom she deliberately encourages to repeat his shortcoming. In placing her child under the discipline of consequences, the mother must use much tact and discretion. In many cases, the natural consequence of the child's fault is precisely that which it is her business to avert, while, at the same time, she looks about for some consequence related to the fault which shall have an educative bearing on the child: for instance, if a boy neglects his studies, the natural consequences is that he remains ignorant; but to allow him to do so would be criminal neglect on the part of the parent.

II. The Habits of Application, Etc.

Rapid Mental Effort—The habits of mental activity and of application are trained by the very means employed to cultivate that of attention. The child may plod diligently through his work who might be trained to rapid mental effort. The teacher herself must be alert, must expect instant answers, quick thought, rapid work. The tortoise will lag behind the hare, but the tortoise must be trained to move, every day, a trifle quicker. Aim steadily at securing quickness of apprehension and execution, and that goes far towards getting it.

Zeal must be Stimulated.—So of application. The child must not be allowed to get into the mood

[page 150]

in which he says, 'Oh, I am so tired of sums,' or 'of history.' His zeal must be stimulated; and there must be always a pleasing vista before him; and the steady, untiring application to work should be held up as honourable, while fitful, flagging attention and effort are scouted.

III. The Habit of Thinking

'A Lion' Operations included in Thinking.—The actual labour of the brain is known to psychologists under various names, and divided into various operations: let us call it thinking, which, for educational purposes, is sufficiently exact; but, by 'thinking,' let us mean a real conscious effort of mind, and not the fancies that flit without effort through the brain. This sort of thing, for instance, an example quoted by Archbishop Thompson in his Laws of Thought [This example, offered by so able a psychologist, is so admirable that I venture to quote it more than once]

:—"when Captain Head was travelling across the pampas of South America, his guide one day suddenly stopped him, and pointing high into the air, cried out 'A lion!' Surprised at such an exclamation, accompanied with such an act, he turned up his eyes, and with difficulty perceived, at an immeasurable height, a flight of condors, soaring in circles in a particular spot. Beneath this spot, far out of sight of himself of himself or guide, lay the carcass of a horse, and over that carcass stood, as the guide well knew, a lion, whom the condors were eyeing with envy from their airy height. The signal of the birds was to him what the sight of the lion alone would have been to the traveller—a full assurance of its existence.

[page 151]
Here was an act of thought which cost the thinker no trouble, which was easy to him as to cast his eyes upward, yet which from us, unaccustomed to the subject, would require many steps and some labour. The sight of the condors convinced him that there was some carcass or other; but as they kept wheeling far above it, instead of swooping down to their feast, he guessed that some beast had anticipated them. Was it a dog, or a jackal? No; the condors would not fear to drive away, or share with, either: it must be some large beast, and as there were lions in the neighbourhood, he concluded that one was here." And all these steps of thought are summed in the words 'A lion.'

This is the sort of thing that the children should go through, more or less, in every lesson—a tracing of effect from cause, or of cause from effect; a comparing of things to find out wherein they are alike, and wherein they differ; a conclusion as to causes or consequences from certain premises.

IV. The Habit of Imagining

The Sense of Incongruous.—All their lessons will afford some scope for some slight exercise of the children's thinking power, some more and some less, and the lessons must be judiciously alternated, so that the more mechanical efforts succeed the more strictly intellectual, and that the pleasing exercise of the imagination, again, succeed efforts of reason. By the way, it is a pity when the sense of the ludicrous is cultivated in children's books at the expense of better things. Alice in Wonderland is a delicious feast of absurdities, which none of us, old or young, could

[page 152]
afford to spare; but it is doubtful whether the child who reads it has the delightful imaginings, the realising of the unknown, with which he reads The Swiss Family Robinson.

This point is worth considering in connection with Christmas books for the little people. Books of 'comicalities' cultivate no power but the sense of the incongruous; and though life is the more amusing for the possession of such a sense, when cultivated to excess it is apt to show itself a flippant habit. Diogenes and the Naughty Boys of Troy is irresistible, but it is not the sort of thing the children will live over and over, and 'play at' by the hour, as we have all played at Robinson Crusoe finding the footprints.

They must have 'funny books,' but do not give the children too much nonsense reading.

Commonplace Tales: Tales of Imagination—Stories, again, of the Christmas holidays, of George and Lucy, of the amusements, foibles, and virtues of children in their own condition of life, leave nothing to the imagination. The children know all about everything so well that it never occurs to them to play at the situations in any one of these tales, or even to read it twice over. But the them have tales of the imagination, scenes laid in other lands and other times, heroic adventures, hairbreadth escapes, delicious fairy tales in which they are never roughly pulled up by the impossible—even where all is impossible, and they know it, and yet believe.

Imagination and Great Conceptions.—And this, not for the children's amusement merely: it is not impossible that posterity may write us down a generation blest with little imagination, and, by so far, the less capable of great conceptions and heroic

[page 153]

efforts, for it is only as we have it in us to let a person or a cause fill the whole stage of the mind, to the exclusion of self-occupation, that we are capable of large-hearted action on behalf of that person or cause. Our novelists say there is nothing left to imagine; and that, therefore, a realistic description of things as they are is all that is open to them. But imagination is nothing if not creative, unless it see, not only what is apparent, but what is conceivable, and what is poetically fit in given circumstances.

Imagination Grows.—Now imagination does not descend, full grown, to take possession of an empty house; like every other power of the mind, it is the merest germ of a power to begin with, and grows by what it gets; and childhood, the age of faith, is the time for its nourishing. The children should have the joy of living in far lands, in other persons, in other times—a delightful double existence; and this joy they will find, for the most part, in their story books. Their lessons, too, history and geography, should cultivate their conceptive powers. If the child do not live in the times of his history lesson, be not at home in the climes of his geography book describes, why, these lessons will fail of their purpose. But let lessons do their best, and the picture gallery of the imagination is poorly hung if the child have not found his way into the realms of fancy.

Thinking comes by Practice.—How the children's various lessons should be handled so as to induce habits of thinking, we shall consider later; but this for the present: thinking, like writing or skating, comes by practice. The child who has never thought, never does think, and probably never will think; for

[page 154]

are there not people enough who go through the world without any deliberate exercise of their own wits? The child must think, get at the reason why of things for himself, every day of his life, and more each day than the day before. Children and parents both are given to invert this educational process. The child asks 'Why?' and the parent answers, rather proud of this evidence of thought in his child. There is some slight show of speculation even in wondering 'Why?' but it is the slightest and most superficial effort the thinking brain produces. Let the parent ask 'Why?' and the child produce the answer, if he can. After he has turned the matter over and over in his mind, there is no harm in telling him—and he will remember it—the reason why. Every walk should offer some knotty problem for the children to think out—"Why does that leaf float on the water, and this pebble sink?" and so on.

V. The Habit of Remembering

Remembering and Recollecting.—Memory is the storehouse of whatever knowledge we possess; and it is upon the fact of the stores lodged in the memory that we take rank as intelligent beings. The children learn in order that they may remember. Much of what we have learned and experienced in childhood, and later, we cannot reproduce, and yet it has formed the groundwork of after knowledge; later notions and opinions have grown out of what we once learned and knew. That is our sunk capital, of which we enjoy the interest though we are unable to realise. Again, much that we have learned and experienced is not only retained

[page 155]

in the storehouse of memory, but is our available capital, we can reproduce, recollect upon demand. This memory which may be drawn upon by the act of recollection is our most valuable endowment.

A 'Spurious' Memory. There is a third kind of (spurious) memory—facts and ideas floating in the brain which yet make no part of it, and are exuded at a single effort; as when a barrister produces all his knowledge of case in his brief, and then forgets to tell about it; or when the schoolboy 'crams' for an examination, writes down what he has thus learned, and behold, it is gone from his gaze for ever: as Ruskin puts it, "They cram to pass, and not to know, they do pass, and they don't know." That this barrister, the physician, should be able thus to dismiss the case on which he has ceased to be occupied, the publisher the book he has rejected, is well for him, and this art of forgetting is not without its uses: but what of the schoolboy who has little left after a year's work but his place in a class list?

Memory a Record in the Brain Substance.—To say anything adequate on the subject of memory is impossible here; but let us try to answer two or three queries which present themselves on the surface. How do we come to 'remember' at all? How do we gain the power to utilise remembered facts—that is, to recollect? And under what conditions is knowledge acquired that neither goes to the growth of brain and mind, nor is available on demand, but is lightly lodged in the brain for some short period, and is then evacuated at a single throw? We are interested in a wonderful invention—an instrument which records spoken words, and

[page 156]

will deliver, say a century hence, speech or lecture on the very words and in the very tones of the speaker. Such an instrument is that function of the brain called memory, whereby the impressions received by the brain are recorded mechanically—at least, such is the theory pretty generally received now by physiologists. That is, the mind takes cognisance of certain facts, and the nerve substance of the brain records that cognisance.

Made under what Conditions.—Now, the questions arise, Under what conditions is such an imprint of fact or event made upon the substance of the brain? Is the record permanent? And is the brain capable of receiving an indefinite number of such impressions? It appears, both from common experience and from an infinite number of examples quoted by psychologists, that any object or idea which is regarded with attention makes the sort of impression on the brain which is said to fix it in the memory. In other words, give an instant's undivided attention to anything whatsoever, and that thing will be remembered.

In describing this effect, the common expression is accurate beyond its intention. We say, "Such and such a sight or sound, or sensation, made a strong impression on me." And that is precisely what has happened: arrest the attention upon any fact or incident, that fact or incident is remembered; it is impressed, imprinted upon the brain substance. The inference is plain. You want a child to remember? Then secure his whole attention, the fixed gaze of his mind, as it were, upon the fact to be remembered; then he will have it: by a sort of photographic (!) process, that fact or idea is 'taken' by his brain, and when he is

[page 157]
an old man, perhaps, the memory of it will flash across him.

Recollection and the Law of Association.—*But it is not enough to have a recollection flash across one incidentally; we want to have the power of recalling at will: and for this, something more is necessary than an occasional act of attention producing a solitary impression. Supposing, for instance, that by good teaching you secure the child's attention to the verb avoir, he will remember it; that is to say, some infinitely slight growth of brain tissue will record and retain that one French verb. But one verb is nothing; you want the child to learn French, and for this you must not only fix his attention upon each new lesson, but each must be so linked into the last that it is impossible for him to recall one without the other following in its train. The physical effect of such a method appears to be that each new growth of the brain tissue is, so to speak, laid upon the last; that is, to put it figuratively, a certain tract of the brain may be conceived of as being overlaid with French. This is to make a practical use of that law of association of ideas of which one would not willingly become the sport; and it is the neglect of this law which invalidates much good teaching. The teacher is content to produce a solitary impression which is only recalled as it is acted upon by a chance suggestion; whereas he should forge all the thinks of a chain to draw his bucket out of the well. Probably the reader may have heard, or heard of, a Dr Pick, who grounded a really philosophical system of mnemonics on these two principles of attention and association. Whatever we may think of his application of it, the principle he asserted is the right one.*

[page 158]

Every Lesson must recall the Last.—Let every lesson gain the child's entire attention, and let each new lesson be so interlaced with the last that the one must recall the other; that again, recalls the one before it, and so on to the beginning.

No Limit to the Recording Power of the Brain.—But the 'lightly come, lightly go' of a mere verbal memory follows no such rules. The child gets his exercise 'by heart,' says it off like a parrot, and behold, it is gone; there is no record of it upon the brain at all. To secure such a record, there must be time; time for that full gaze of the mind we call attention, and for the growth of the brain tissue to the new idea. Given these conditions, there appears to be no limit of quantity to the recording power of the brain. Except in this way: a girl learns French and speaks it fairly well; by the time she is a grandmother she has forgotten it entirely, has not a word left. When this is the case, her French has been disused; she has not been in the habit of reading, hearing, or speaking French from youth to age. Whereby it is evident that, to secure right-of-way to that record of French imprinted on her brain, the path should have been kept open by frequent goings and comings.

But Links of Association a Condition of Recollection.—To acquire any knowledge or power whatsoever, and then to leave it to grow rusty in a neglected corner of the brain, is practically useless. Where there is no chain of association to draw the bucket out of the well, it is all the same as if there were no water there. As to how to form these links, every subject will suggest a suitable method. The child has a lesson about Switzerland to-day, and one about Holland to-morrow, and the one is linked to

[page 159]

the other by the very fact that the two countries have hardly anything in common; what the one has, the other has not. Again, the association will be of similarity, and not of contrast. In our own experience we find that colours, places, sounds, odours recall persons or events; but links of this sensuous order can hardly be employed in education. The link between any two things must be found in the nature of the things associated.

VI. The Habit of Perfect Execution

The Habit of turning out Imperfect Work.—'Throw perfection into all you do' is a counsel upon which a family may be brought up with great advantage. We English, as a nation, think too much of persons, and too little of things, work, execution. Our children are allowed to make their figures or their letters, their stitches, their dolls' clothes, their small carpentry, anyhow, with the notion that they will do better by-and-by. Other nations—the Germans and the French, for instance—look at the question philosophically, and know that if children get the habit of turning out imperfect work, the men and women will undoubtedly keep that habit up. I remember being delighted with the work of a class of about forty children, of six and seven, in an elementary school at Heidelberg. They were doing a writing lesson, accompanied by a good deal of oral teaching from a master, who wrote each word on the blackboard. By-and-by the slates were shown, and I did not observe one faulty or irregular letter on the whole forty slates. The same principle of 'perfection' was to be discerned in a recent exhibition of school-work

[page 160]

held throughout France. No faulty work was shown, to be excused on the plea that it was the work of children.

A Child should Execute Perfectly. No work should be given to a child that he cannot execute perfectly, and then perfection should be required from him as a matter of course. For instance, he is set to do a copy of strokes, and is allowed to show a slateful at all sorts of slopes and all sorts of intervals; his moral sense is vitiated, his eye is injured. Set him six strokes to copy; let him, not bring a slateful, but six perfect strokes, at regular distances and at regular slopes. If he produces a faulty pair, get him to point out the fault, and persevere until he has produced his task; if he does not do it to-day, let him go on to-morrow and the next day, and when the six perfect strokes appear, let it be an occasion of triumph. So with the little tasks of painting, drawing, or construction he sets himself—let everything he does be well done. An unsteady house of cards is a thing to be ashamed of. Closely connected with this habit of 'perfect work' is that of finishing whatever is taken in hand. The child should rarely be allowed to set his hand to a new undertaking until the last is finished.

VII. Some Moral Habits—Obedience

It is disappointing that, in order to cover the ground at all, we must treat those moral habits, which the mother owes it to her children to cultivate in them, in a slight and inadequate way; but the point to be borne in mind is, that all has been already said about the cultivation of habit applies with the greatest possible force to each of these habits.

[page 161]

The Whole Duty of a Child—*First and infinitely the most important, is the habit of obedience. Indeed, obedience is the whole duty of the child, and for this reason—every other duty of the child is fulfilled as a matter of obedience to his parents. Not only so: obedience is the whole duty of man; obedience to conscience, to law, to Divine direction.*

It has been well observed that each of the three recorded temptations of our Lord in the wilderness is a suggestion, not of an act of overt sin, but of an act of wilfulness, that state directly opposed to obedience, and out of which springs all that foolishness which is bound up in the heart of a child.

Obedience no Accidental Duty.—*Now, if the parent realise that obedience is no mere accidental duty, the fulfilling of which is a matter that lies between himself and the child, but that he is the appointed agent to train the child up to the intelligent obedience of the self-compelling, law-abiding human being, he will see that he has no right to forego the obedience of his child, and that every act of disobedience in the child is a direct condemnation of the parent. Also, he will see that the motive of the child's obedience is not the arbitrary one of, 'Do this, or that, because I have said so,' but the motive of the apostolic injunction, "Children, obey your parents in the Lord, for this is right."*

Children must have the Desire to Obey.—*It is only in proportion as the will of the child is in the act of obedience, and he obeys because his sense of right makes him desire to obey in spite of temptations to disobedience—not of constraint, but willingly—that the habit has been formed which will, hereafter, enable the child to use the strength of his will against*

[page 162]

his inclinations when these prompt him to lawless courses. It is said that the children of parents who are most strict in exacting obedience often turn out ill; and that orphans and other poor waifs brought up under strict discipline only wait their opportunity to break into license. Exactly so; because, in these cases, there is no gradual training of the child in the habit of obedience; no gradual enlisting of his will on the side of sweet service and a free will offering of submission to the highest law: the poor children are simply bullied into submission to the will, that is, the wilfulness, of another; not at all, 'for it is right'; only because it is convenient.

Expect Obedience.—The mother has no more sacred duty than that of training her infant to instant obedience. To do so is no difficult task; the child is still "trailing clouds of glory...from God, who is his home"; the principle of obedience is within him, waiting to be called into exercise. There is no need to rate the child, or threaten him, or use any manner of violence, because the parent is invested with authority which the child intuitively recognises. It is enough to say, 'Do this,' in a quiet, authoritative tone, and expect it to be done. The mother often loses her hold over children because they detect in the tone of her voice that she does not expect them obey her behests; she does not think enough of her position; has not sufficient confidence in her own authority. The mother's great stronghold is in the habit of obedience. If she begin by requiring that her children always obey her, why, they will always do so as a matter of course; but let them once get the thin end of the wedge in, let them discover that they can do otherwise than obey, and a woeful struggle

[page 163]

begins, which commonly ends in the children doing that which is right in their own eyes.

This is the sort of thing which is fatal: The children are in the drawing room, and a caller is announced. 'You must go upstairs now.' 'Oh, mother dear, do let us stay in the window-corner; we will be as quiet as mice!' The mother is rather proud of her children's pretty manners, and they stay. They are not quiet, of course; but that is the least of the evils; they have succeeded in doing as they chose and not as they were bid, and they will not put their necks under the yoke again without a struggle. It is in little matters that the mother is worsted. 'Bedtime, Willie!' 'Oh, mamma, just let me finish this'; and the mother yields, forgetting that the case in point is of no consequence; the thing that matters is that the child should be daily confirming a habit of obedience by the unbroken repetition of acts of obedience. It is astonishing how clever the child is in finding ways of evading the spirit while he observes the letter. 'Mary, come in.' 'Yes, mother'; but her mother calls four times before Mary comes. 'Put away your bricks'; and the bricks are put away with slow reluctant fingers. 'You must always wash your hands when you hear the first bell.' The child obeys for that once, and no more.

To avoid these displays of wilfulness, the m other will insist from the first on an obedience which is prompt, cheerful, and lasting—save for lapses of memory on the child's part. Tardy, unwilling, occasional obedience is hardly worth the having; and it is greatly easier to give the child the habit of perfect obedience by never allowing him in anything else, than it is to obtain this mere formal obedience by a

[page 164]

constant exercise of authority. By-and-by, when he is old enough, take the child into confidence; let him know what a noble thing it is to be able to make himself do, in a minute, and brightly, the very thing he would rather not do. To secure this habit of obedience, the mother must exercise great self-restraint; she must never give a command which she does not intend to see carried out to the full. And she must not lay upon her children burdens, grievous to be borne, of command heaped upon command.

Law Ensures Liberty.—The children who are trained to perfect obedience may be trusted with a good deal of liberty: they receive a few directions which they know they must not disobey; and for the rest, they are left to learn how to direct their own actions, even at the cost of some small mishaps; and are not pestered with a perpetual fire of 'Do this' and 'Don't do that!'

VIII.—Truthfulness

It is unnecessary to say a word of the duty of Truthfulness; but the training of the child in the habit of strict veracity is another matter, and one which requires delicate care and scrupulosity on the part of the mother.

Three Causes of Lying—All Vicious.—The vice of lying causes: carelessness in ascertaining the truth, carelessness in stating the truth, and a deliberate intention to deceive. That all three are vicious, is evident from the fact that a man's character may be ruined by what is no more than a careless mis-statement on the part of another; the speaker repeats a damaging remark without taking

[page 165]
the trouble to sift it; or he repeats what he has heard or seen with so little care to deliver the truth that his statement becomes no better than a lie.

Only One Kind visited on Children.—Now, of the three kinds of lying, it is only, as a matter of fact, the third which is severely visited upon the child; the first and the second he is allowed in. He tells you he has seen 'lots' of spotted dogs in the town—he has really seen two; that 'all the boys' are collecting crests—he knows of three who are doing so; that 'everybody' says Jones is a 'sneak'—the fact is he has heard Brown say so. These departures from strict veracity are no matters of such slight importance that the mother is apt to let them pass as the 'children's chatter'; but, indeed, ever such lapse is damaging to the child's sense of truth—a blade which easily loses its keenness of edge.

Accuracy of Statement.—The mother who trains her child to strict accuracy of statement about things small and great fortifies him against temptations to the grosser forms of lying; he will not readily colour a tale to his own advantage, suppress facts, equivocate, when the statement of the simple fact has become a binding habit, and when he has not been allowed to form the contrary vicious habit of playing fast and loose with words.

Exaggeration and Ludicrous Embellishments.—Two forms of prevarication, very tempting to the child, will require great vigilance on the mother's part—that of exaggeration and that of clothing a story with ludicrous embellishments. However funny a circumstance may be as described by the child, the ruthless mother must strip the tale of everything over and above the naked truth: for, indeed, a reputation

[page 166]
for facetiousness is dearly purchased by the loss of that dignity of character, in child or man, which accompanies the habit of strict veracity; it is possible, happily, to be humorous, without any sacrifice of truth.

Reverence, etc.—As for reverence, consideration for others, respect for persons and property, I can only urge the importance of a sedulous cultivation of these moral qualities—the distinguishing marks of a refined nature—until they become the daily habits of the child's life; and the more, because a self-assertive, aggressive, self-seeking temper is but too characteristic of the times we live in.

Temper—Born in a Child.—I am anxious, however, to a say a few words on the habit of sweet temper. It is very customary to regard temper as constitutional, that which is born in you and is neither to be helped nor hindered. 'Oh, she is a good-tempered little soul; nothing puts her out!' 'Oh, he has his father's temper; the least thing that goes contrary makes him fly into a passion,' are the sorts of remarks we hear constantly.

Not Temper, but Tendency.—It is no doubt true that children inherit a certain tendency to irascibility or to amiability, to fretfulness, discontentment, peevishness, sullenness, murmuring, and impatience; or to cheerfulness, trustfulness, good-humour, patience, and humility. It is also true that upon the preponderance of any of these qualities—upon temper, that is—the happiness of wretchedness of child and man depends, as well as the comfort or misery of the people who live with him. We all know people possessed of integrity and of many excellent virtues who make themselves intolerable to

[page 167]

their belongings. The root of evil is, not that these people were born sullen, or peevish, or envious—that might have been mended; but that they were permitted to grow up in these dispositions. Here, if anywhere, the power of habit is invaluable: it rests with the parents to correct the original twist, all the more so if it is from them the child gets it, and to send their child into the world best with an even, happy temper, inclined to make the best of things, to look on the bright side, to impute the best and kindest motives to others, and to make no extravagant claims on his own account—fertile source of ugly tempers. And this, because the child is born with no more than certain tendencies.

Parents must correct Tendency by New Habit of Temper.—It is by force of habit that a tendency becomes a temper; and it rests with the mother to hinder the formation of ill tempers, to force that of good tempers. Nor is it difficult to do this while the child's countenance is as an open book to his mother, and she reads the thoughts of his heart before he is aware of them himself. Remembering that every envious, murmuring, discontented thought leaves a track in the very substance of the child's brain for such thoughts to run in again and again—that this track, this rut, so to speak, is ever widening and deepening with the traffic in ugly thoughts—the mother's care is to hinder at the outset the formation of any such track. She sees into her child's soul—sees the evil temper in the act of rising: now is her opportunity.

Change the Child's Thoughts.—Let her change the child's thoughts before ever the bad temper has had time to develop into conscious feeling, much less

[page 168]

act: take him out of doors, send him to fetch or carry, tell him or show him something of interest,—in a word, give him something else to think about; but all in a natural way, and without letting the child perceive that he is being treated. As every fit of sullenness leaves place in the child's mind for another fit of sullenness to succeed it, so every such fit averted by the mother's tact tends to obliterate the evil traces of former sullen tempers. At the same time, the mother is careful to lay down a highway for the free course of all sweet and genial thoughts and feelings.

I have been offering suggestions, not for a course of intellectual and moral training, but only for the formation of certain habits which should be, as it were, the outworks of character. Even with this limited programme, I have left unnoticed many matters fully as important as those touched upon. In the presence of an embarrassment of riches, it has been necessary to adopt some principle of selection; and I have thought it well to dwell upon considerations which do not appear to me to have their full weight with educated parents, rather than upon those of which every thoughtful person recognises the force.

CHAPTER 12.
HISTORY: IS IT BORING AND DRY?

WHY TEACH HISTORY?

Have you ever wondered about the value of teaching history?

What relevance does it have to us today?

After all, isn't history just a dry, boring list of irrelevant dates?

And what on earth can we learn from people who have already lived their lives and are dead?

3 EXCELLENT REASONS TO TEACH HISTORY

I've got some very interesting thoughts on the question of 'why?' here from three different people.

The first person is George Santanyana. He was a Spanish-American philosopher, essayist, poet, and novelist. The second person is Winston Churchill who was a statesman, a British politician and the Prime Minister during World War Two. He was also an artist, a writer and a great historian. And the third person is someone you are quite familiar with; our dear friend and teacher, Charlotte Mason.

1. George Santayana wrote in his book, *The Life of Reason*: "Those who cannot remember the past are condemned to repeat it."

2. Winston Churchill said: "The greatest advances in human civilization have come when we recovered what we had lost: when we learned the lessons of history"

3. Charlotte Mason wrote in Volume 6, *A Philosophy of Education*, p. 179: *...it is necessary to know something of what has gone before in order to think justly of what is occurring today.* And she also wrote: "A Philosophy of Education" p. 169: *...offer such a*

liberal and generous diet of history to every child in the country as shall give weight to his decisions, consideration to his actions and stability to his conduct; that stability, the lack of which has plunged us into many a stormy sea of unrest.

THREE GUIDELINES FOR TEACHING HISTORY

1. Be enthusiastic yourself and teach what you love.

A friend of mine, (let's call her Linda) told me of a teacher she had when she was nine, who made history so alive for her, so that she loved reading all the historical novels she could find. When Linda went on to Middle School at age 11, her new history teacher almost stifled all interest by presenting the subject in a dry, uninteresting way.

Linda went on to become a teacher herself when she grew up.

Then, guess what! Linda actually had to teach history to 11 and 12 year-olds herself!

Suddenly, Linda found that the glory of those early discoveries started to come back to her. She said she realised that she didn't need to teach in the way that she had been taught in Intermediate, but that she could teach history in an alive, exciting way. She became enthusiastic.

She was enthusiastic about:

- The costumes for their richness and variety,
- The architecture telling of the soaring visions of those who glorified either their Creator or themselves,
- The place of the Bible in the history of mankind
- The different civilizations she learnt about and taught about.

Linda got enthusiastic. And it paid off. She was a popular and successful history teacher and her students loved history.

2. Choose your books wisely.

Charlotte Mason said:

For the matter for this intelligent teaching of history, eschew, in the first place, nearly all history books written expressly for children... Volume 1, page 281.

I love that comment! That word, 'eschew' means: avoid, have nothing to do with, shun, turn your back on, steer clear of.

Charlotte Mason didn't like most history books written for children. I wonder what she would think of modern books written for children? She was certainly not a fan of the latest tendency to 'dumb down' information.

Another comment on how to teach history, from Charlotte Mason:

... let them get the spirit of history into them by reading, at least, one old Chronicle written by a man who saw and knew something of what he wrote about, and did not get it at secondhand. Volume 1, page 282.

Here, Charlotte Mason is again encouraging us to allow the masters speak to our children without interference from you and me, the teachers. She is saying to refer to texts written at the time that the history was occurring, because this is first-hand information. An interesting perspective, isn't it?

3. Don't try to teach everything.

Charlotte Mason said:

The fatal mistake is in the notion that he must learn 'outlines', or a baby edition of the whole history of England, or of Rome, just as he must cover the geography of all the world. Let him, on the contrary, linger pleasantly over the history of a single man, a short period, until he thinks the thoughts of that man, is at home in the ways of that period. Though he is reading and thinking of the lifetime of a single man, he is really getting intimately acquainted with the history of a whole nation for a whole age. Volume 1, page 280

I think this is quite an interesting quotation, especially given the penchant in modern homeschool circles to try and teach the whole of human history in a sort of sweeping overview. This usually means that people are reading books which are what Charlotte Mason called "outlines".

Charlotte Mason's recommendation was to concentrate on a single period of history and get to know all about it. She said there is no need to try to cover the whole of history, but to enjoy getting to know a single man (or woman).

I remember when one of my daughters became deeply involved in Elizabethan history. She loved Elizabeth I. She could quote chunks of speeches made by Elizabeth. She knew the intricacies of court, and was very knowledgeable about fashion and fabrics of the time. She read many books about

Elizabeth and her times. And she collected historical novels set in Elizabethan times. She went on to study history at university and was offered post-graduate study in history.

She learnt about other periods of history, and often added dates and personalities to her history timeline and history book, but Elizabethan England remained her favourite period.

This may challenge you to reconsider how and if you teach history to your children.

SUMMARY

In this chapter I have given you three excellent reasons to teach history. And I've given you three rules to guide you in teaching history. I've included quotations from Charlotte Mason, and hopefully, I've encouraged you to see that you really don't have to do it all.

ASSIGNMENT

The reading today is a bit longer than usual. I spent quite a while choosing what to include, and I do believe that all I've included is relevant and interesting, so I encourage you to persist and complete your reading this chapter.

Read a chapter from Charlotte Mason on the teaching of history. Volume One pages 279 – 295. I am including it here for you.

SUPPLEMENT

Volume 1, pages 279 – 295

XVIII.—HISTORY

A Storehouse of Ideas

Much that has been said about the teaching of geography applies equally to that of history. Here, too, is a subject which should be to the child an inexhaustible storehouse of ideas, should enrich the chambers of his House Beautiful with a thousand tableaux, pathetic and heroic, and should form in him, insensibly, principles whereby he will hereafter judge of the behaviour of nations, and will rule his own conduct as one of a nation.

This is what the study of history should do for the child; but what is he to get out of the miserable little chronicle of feuds, battles, and death which is presented to him by way of 'a reign'—all the more repellent because it bristles with dates?

As for the dates, they never come right; the tens and units he can get, but the centuries will go astray; and how is he to put the right events in the right reign, when, to him, one king differs from another only in number, one period from another only in date?

But he blunders through with it; reads in his pleasant, chatty little history book all the reigns of all the kings, from William the Conqueror to William IV., and back to the dim days of British rule. And with what result? This: that, possibly, no way of warping the judgment of the child, of filling him with crude notions, narrow prejudices, is more successful than that of carrying him through some such course of English history; and all the more so if his little text-book be moral or religious in tone, and undertake to point the moral as well as to record the fact.

Moral teaching falls, no doubt, within the province of history; but the one small volume which the child uses affords no scope for the fair and reasonable discussion upon which moral decisions should be based, nor is the child old enough to be put into the judicial attitude which such a decision supposes.

'Outlines' Mischievous

The fatal mistake is in the notion that he must learn 'outlines,' or a baby edition of the whole history of England, or of Rome, *just as he must cover the geography of all the world. Let him, on the contrary, linger pleasantly over the history of a single man, a short period, until he thinks the thoughts of that man, is at home in the ways of that period. Though he is reading and thinking of the lifetime of a single man, he is really getting intimately acquainted with the history of a whole nation for a whole age. Let him spend a year of happy intimacy with Alfred, 'the truth-teller,' with the Conqueror, with Richard and Saladin, or with Henry V.—Shakespeare's Henry V.—and his victorious army.*

Let him know the great people and the common people, the ways of the court and of the crowd. Let him know what other nations were doing while we at home were doing thus and thus. If he come to think that the people of another age were truer, larger-hearted, simpler-minded than ourselves, that the people of some other land were, at one time, at any rate, better than we, why, so much the better for him.

So are most History Books written for Children—For the matter for this intelligent teaching of history, eschew, in the first place, nearly all history books written expressly for children; and in the next place, all compendiums, outlines, abstracts whatsoever.

For the abstracts, considering what part the study of history is fitted to play in the education of the child, there is not a word to be said in their favour; and as for what are called children's books, the children of educated parents are able to understand history written with literary power, and are not attracted by the twaddle of reading-made-easy little history books. Given judicious skipping, and a good deal of the free paraphrasing mothers are so ready at, and the children may be taken through the first few volumes of a well-written, illustrated, popular history of England, say as far as the Tudors. In the course of such reading a good deal of questioning into them, and questioning out of them, will be necessary, both to secure their attention and to fix the facts.

This is the least that should be done; but better than this would be fuller information, more graphic details about two or three early epochs.

Early History of a Nation best fitted for Children

The early history of a nation is far better fitted than its later records for the study of children, because the story moves on a few broad, simple lines; while statesmanship, so far as it exists, is no more than the efforts of a resourceful mind to cope with circumstances. Mr. Freeman has provided interesting early English history for children; but is it not on the whole better to take them straight to the fountainhead, where possible? In these early years, while there are no examinations ahead, and the children may yet go leisurely, let them get the spirit of history into them by reading, at least, one old Chronicle written by a man who saw and knew something of what he wrote about, and did not get it at second-hand. These old books are easier and pleasanter reading than most modern works on history, because the writers know little of the 'dignity of history'; they purl along pleasantly as a forest brook, tell you 'all about it,' stir your heart with the story of a great event, amuse you with pageants and shows, make you intimate with the great people, and friendly with the lowly. They are just the right thing for the children whose eager souls want to get at the living people behind the words of the history book, caring nothing at all about progress, or statutes, or about anything but the persons, for whose action history is, to the child's mind, no more than a convenient stage. A child who has been carried through a single old chronicler in this way has a better foundation for all historical training than if he knew all the dates and names and facts that ever were crammed for examination.

Some old Chronicles

First in order of time, and full of the most captivating reading, is the Ecclesiastical History of England (see Appendix A) of the Venerable Bede, who, writing of himself so early as the seventh century, says, "It was always sweet to me to learn, to teach, and to write." "He has left us," says Professor Morley, "a history of the early years of England, succinct, yet often warm with life; business-like, and yet childlike in its tone; at once practical and spiritual, simply just, and the work of a true scholar, breathing love to God and man.

We owe to Bede alone the knowledge of much that is most interesting in our early history." William of Malmesbury (twelfth century) says of Bede, "That almost all knowledge of past events was buried in the same grave with him"; and he is no bad judge, for in his Chronicles of the Kings of England he himself is considered to have carried to perfection the art of chronicle-making. He is especially vivid and graphic about contemporary events-the story of the dreary civil war of Stephen and Matilda.

Meantime, there is Asser, who writes the life of Alfred, whose friend and fellow-worker he is. "It seems to me right," he says, "to explain a little more fully what I have heard from my lord Alfred." He tells us how, "When I had come into his presence at the royal villa, called Leonaford, I was honourably received by him, and remained that time with him at his court about eight months, during which I read to him whatever books he liked, and such as he had at hand; for this is his most usual custom, both night and day, amid his many other occupations of mind and body, either himself to read books or to listen whilst others read them."

When he was not present to see for himself, as at the battle of Ashdown, Asser takes pains to get the testimony of eyewitnesses. "But Alfred, as we have been told by those who were present and would not tell an untruth, marched up promptly, with his men to give them battle; for King Ethelred remained a long time in his tent in prayer."

Then there are Chronicles of the Crusades, contemporary narratives of the crusades of Richard Coeur de Lion, by Richard of Devizes, and Geoffrey de Vinsany, and of the crusade of St. Louis, by Lord John de Joinville.

It is needless to extend the list; one such old chronicle in a year, or the suitable bits of one such chronicle, and the child's imagination is aglow, his mind is teeming with ideas; he has had speech of those who have themselves seen and heard; and the matter-of-fact way in which the old monks tell their tales is exactly what children prefer. Afterwards, you may put any dull outlines into their hands, and they will make history for themselves.

Age of Myths

But every nation has its heroic age before authentic history begins: these were giants in the land in those days, and the child wants to know about them. He has every right to revel in such classic myths as we possess as a nation; and to land him in a company of painted savages, by way of giving him his first introduction to his people, is a little hard; it is to make his vision of the past harsh and bald as a Chinese painting. But what is to be done?

If we ever had an Homeric age, have we not, being a practical people, lost all record thereof? Here is another debt that we owe to those old monkish chroniclers: the echoes of some dim, rich past had come down to, at any rate, the twelfth century: they fell upon the ear of a Welsh priest, one Geoffrey of Monmouth; and while William of Malmesbury was writing his admirable History of the Kings of England, what does Geoffrey do but weave the traditions of the people into an orderly History of the British Kings, reaching back all the way to King Brut, the grandson of Aeneas. How he came to know about kings, that no other historian had heard of, is a matter that he is a little roguish about; he got it all, he says, out of "that book in the British language which Walter, Archdeacon of Oxford, brought out of Britainy."

Be that as it may, here we read of Gorboduc, King Lear, Merlin, Uther Pendragon, and, best of all, of King Arthur, the writer making 'the little finger of his Arthur stouter than the back of Alexander the Great.' Here is, indeed, a treasure-trove which the children should be made free of ten years before they come to read the Idylls of the King.

Some caution must, however, be exercised in reading Geoffrey of Monmouth. His tales of marvel are delightful; but when he quits the marvellous and romances freely about historical facts and personages, he becomes a bewildering guide.

Many of these 'chronicles,' written in Latin by the monks, are to be had in readable English; the only caution to be observed is, that the mother should run her eye over the pages before she reads them aloud. (Bohn's Antiquarian Library [5s. a volume] includes Bede, William of Malmesbury, Dr. Giles's Six Old English Chronicles—Asser and Geoffrey of Monmouth being two of them—Chronicles of the Crusaders, etc.)

Froissart, again, most delightful of chroniclers, himself 'tame' about the court of Queen Phillippa, when he chose to be in England—from whom else should the child get the story of the French wars? And so of as much else as there is time for; the principle being, that, whenever practicable, the child should get his first notions of a given period, not from the modern historian, the commentator and reviewer, but from the original sources of history, the writings of contemporaries. The mother must, however, exercise discrimination in her choice of early 'Chronicles,' as all are not equally reliable.

Plutarch's 'Lives.'

In the same way, readings from Plutarch's Lives will afford the best preparation for the study of Grecian or of Roman history. Alexander the Great is something more than a name to the child who reads this sort of thing:—

"When the horse Bucephalus was offered in sale to Philip, at the price of thirteen talents (= £2518, 15s.), the king, with the prince and many others, went into the field to see some trial made of him. The horse appeared very vicious and unmanageable, and was so far from suffering himself to be mounted, that he would not bear to be spoken to, but turned fiercely upon all the grooms.

Philip was displeased at their bringing him so wild and ungovernable a horse, and bade them take him away. But Alexander, who had observed him well, said, 'What a horse they are losing for want of skill and spirit to manage him!'

"Philip at first took no notice of this; but upon the prince's often repeating the same expression, and showing great uneasiness, he said, 'Young man, you find fault with your elders as if you knew more than they, or could manage the horse better.'

"'And I certainly could,' answered the prince.

"'If you should not be able to ride him, what forfeiture will you submit for your rashness?'

"Upon this all the company laughed; but the king and prince agreeing as to the forfeiture, Alexander ran to the horse, and laying hold on the bridle, turned him to the sun, for he had observed, it seems, that the shadow which fell before the horse, and continually moved as he moved, greatly disturbed him.

While his fierceness and fury lasted, the kept speaking to him softly and stroking him; after which he gently let fall his mantle, leaped lightly upon his back, and got his seat very safe. Then, without pulling the reins too hard, or using either whip or spur, he set him agoing. As soon as he perceived his uneasiness abated, and that he wanted only to run, he put him in a full gallop, and pushed him on both with the voice and spur.

"Philip and all his court were in great distress for him at first, and a profound silence took place; but when the prince had turned him and brought him safe back, they all received him with loud exclamations, except his father, who wept for joy, and kissing him, said 'Seek another kingdom, my son, that may be worthy of thy abilities, for Macedonia is too small for thee' "

Here, again, in North's inimitable translation, we get the sort of vivid graphic presentation which makes 'History' as real to the child as are the adventures of Robinson Crusoe.

To sum up, to know as much as they may about even one short period, is far better for the children than to know the 'outlines' of all history.

And in the second place, children are quite able to take in intelligent ideas in intelligent language, and should by no means be excluded from the best that is written on the period they are about.

History Books

It is not at all easy to choose the right history books for children. Mere summaries of facts must, as we have seen, be eschewed; and we must be equally careful to avoid generalisations.

The natural function of the mind, in the early years of life, is to gather the material of knowledge with a view to that very labour of generalisation which is proper to the adult mind; a labour which we should all carry on to some extent for ourselves.

As it is, our minds are so poorly furnished that we accept the conclusions presented to us without demur; but we can, at any rate, avoid giving children cut-and-dried opinions upon the course of history while they are yet young. What they want is graphic details concerning events and persons upon which imagination goes to work; and opinions tend to form themselves by slow degrees as knowledge grows.

Mr York Powell has, perhaps more than others, hit upon the right teaching for the young children I have in view. In the preface to his Old Stories from British History,[1] he says:—"The writer has chosen such stories as he thought would amuse and please his readers, and give them at the same time some knowledge of the lives and thoughts of their forefathers. To this end he has not written solely of great folk—kings and queens and generals—but also of plain people and children, ay, and birds and beasts too"; and we get the tale of King Lear and of Cuculain, and of King Canute and the poet Otter, of Havelock and Ubba, and many more, all brave and glorious stories; indeed, Mr York Powell gives us a perfect treasure-trove in his two little volumes of Old Stories and Sketches from British History,[1] which are the better for our purpose, because children can read them for themselves so soon as they are able to read at all.

These tales, written in good and simple English, and with a certain charm of style, lend themselves admirably to narration.

Indeed, it is most interesting to hear children of seven or eight go through a long story without missing a detail, putting every event in its right order. These narrations are never a slavish reproduction of the original.

A child's individuality plays about what he enjoys, and the story comes from his lips, not precisely as the author tells it, but with a certain spirit and colouring which express the narrator.

By the way, it is very important that children should be allowed to narrate in their own way, and should not be pulled up or helped with words and expressions from the text.

A narration should be original as it comes from the child— that is, his own mind should have acted upon the matter it has received.

Narrations which are mere feats of memory are quite valueless.

I have already spoken of the sorts of old chronicles upon which children should be nourished; but these are often too diffuse to offer good matter for narration, and it is well to have quite fitting short tales for this purpose.

I should like to mention two other little volumes in which children delight, which feed patriotic sentiment and lay a broad basis for historical knowledge.

I mean Mrs Frewen Lord's Tales from St Paul's 1. It is a beautiful and delightful thing to take children informed by these tales to the Abbey or St Paul's, and let them identify for themselves the spots consecrated to their heroes. They know so much and are so full of vivid interest that their elders stand by instructed and inspired.

There are, no doubt, multitudes of historical tales and sketches for children, and some of them, like Miss Brooke Hunt's Prisoners of the Tower, 1 are very good; but let the mother beware: there is nothing which calls for more delicate tact and understanding sympathy with the children than this apparently simple matter of choosing their lesson-books, and especially, perhaps, their lesson-books in history.

Many children of eight or nine will be quite ready to read with pleasure A History of England, by H.O. Arnold Forster, who has long since won his spurs in the field of educational literature.

In this, as in matters of more immediate statecraft, Mr Arnold Forster has the gift to see a defect and a remedy, an omission and the means of supplying it. He saw that English children grew up without any knowledge of the conditions under which they live, and of the laws which govern them; but since the appearance of The Citizen Reader and The Laws of Every-day Life, we have changed all that.

The History of England, or, as the children call it, History, ignoring the fact that there is any other history than that of England, has hitherto been presented to young people as "outlines of dates and facts, or as collections of romantic stories, with little coherence and less result on the fortunes of the country." Mr Arnold Forster says in his preface that he "is reluctant to introduce his book by any such repellent title as 'A Summary,' or 'An Outline of English History.'

Such titles seem on the face of them to imply that the element of interest and the romance inseparable from the life and doings of individuals are excluded, and that an amplified chronological table has been made to do duty for history.

But to read English history and fail to realise that it is replete with interest, sparkling with episode, and full of dramatic incident, is to miss all the pleasure and most of the instruction which its sturdy, if properly pursued, can give."

The author fulfils his implied promise, and his work is, I venture to say, as "replete with interest, sparkling with episode, and full of dramatic incident" as is possible, considering the limitations imposed upon him by the facts that he writes for uneducated readers, and gives us a survey of the whole of English History in a pleasant, copiously and wisely illustrated volume of some eight hundred pages.

How telling and lucid this is, for example, and how we all wish we had come across such a paragraph in our early studies of architecture:—"On page 23 we have pictures of two windows. One of them is what is called a Pointed window. All the arches in it go up to a point. It was built a long time before the Tudor period. The other was built in the time of Queen Elizabeth. In it the upright shaft, or mullion, of the window goes straight up to the top without forming an arch. This style of building a window is called the Perpendicular Style, because the mullions of the window are 'perpendicular.' Some of the most famous buildings in England built in Tudor times, and in the perpendicular style, are the Chapel of King's College, Cambridge, and Hatfield House, the residence of the Marquis of Salisbury, in Hertfordshire."

Mr Arnold Forster has done in this volume for children and the illiterate, what Professor Green did in his Shorter History of England for somewhat more advanced students, awakening many to the fact that history is an entrancing subject of study. This is a real introduction to real history. The portraits are an especially valuable feature of the work.

Dates

In order to give definiteness to what may soon become a pretty wide knowledge of history—mount a sheet of cartridge-paper and divide it into twenty columns, letting the first century of the Christian era come in the middle, and let each remaining column represent a century B.C. or A.D., as the case may be.

Then let the child himself write, or print, as he is able, the names of the people he comes upon in due order, in their proper century.

We need not trouble ourselves at present with more exact dates, but this simple table of the centuries will suggest a graphic panorama to the child's mind, and he will see events in their time-order.

Illustrations by the Children

History readings afford admirable material for narration, and children enjoy narrating what they have read or heard. They love, too, to make illustrations. Children who had been reading Julius Caesar (and also, Plutarch's Life), were asked to make a picture of their favourite scene, and the results showed the extraordinary power of visualising which the little people possess. Of course that which they visualise, or imagine clearly, they know; it is a life possession.

The drawings of the children in question are psychologically interesting as showing what various and sometimes obscure points appeal to the mind of a child; and also, that children have the same intellectual pleasure as persons of cultivated mind in working out new hints and suggestions. The drawings, be it said, leave much to be desired, but they have this in common with the art of primitive peoples: they tell the tale directly and vividly.

A girl of nine and a half pictures Julius Caesar conquering

Britain. He rides in a chariot mounted on scythes, he is robed in blue, and bits of blue sky here and there give the complementary colour. In the distance, a soldier plants the ensign bearing the Roman eagle, black on a pink ground.

In the foreground, is a hand-to-hand combat between Roman and Briton, each having a sword of enormous length. Other figures are variously employed.

Another, gives us Antony 'making his speech after the death of Caesar.' This girl, who is older, gives us architecture; you look through an arch, which leads into a side street, and, in the foreground, Antony stands on a platform at the head of a flight of marle steps. Antony's attitude expresses indignation and scorn. Below, is a crowd of Romans wearing the toga, whose attitudes show various shades of consternation and dismay.

Behind, is Antony's servant in uniform, holding his master's horse; and on the platform, in the rear of Antony, lies Caesar, with the royal purple thrown over him. The chief value of the drawing, as a drawing, is that it tells the tale.

Another girl draws Calpurnia begging Caesar not to go to the Senate. Caesar stands armed and perturbed, while Carpurnia holds his outstretched hand with both of hers as she kneels before him, her face raised in entreaty; her loose blue night-robe and long golden hair give colour to the picture. This artist is fourteen, and the drawing is better done.

Another artist presents Brutus and Portia in the orchard with a 'south-wall' of red brick, espaliers, and two dignified figures which hardly tell their tale.

Another child gives us the scene in the forum, Caesar seated in royal purple, Brutus kneeling before him, and Casca standing behind his chair with out-stretched hand holding a dagger, saying "Speak, hands, for me," while Caesar says, "Doth not Brutus bootless kneel?"

Again, we get Lucius playing to Brutus in the tent. Brutus, armed cap-a-pie, seated on a stool, is vainly trying to read, while Lucius, a pretty figure, seated before him, plays the harp. The two sentries, also fully armed, are stretched on the floor sound asleep.

Another, gives us Claudius dressed as a woman at the women's festival-the ladies with remarkable eyes, and each carrying a flaming torch.

Another pictures, with great spirit, Caesar reading his history to the conquered Gauls, who stand in rows on the hillside listening to the great man with exemplary patience.

In these original illustrations (several of them by older children than those we have in view here), we get an example of the various images that present themselves to the minds of children during the reading of a great work; and a single such glimpse into a child's mind convinces us of the importance of sustaining that mind upon strong meat. Imagination does not stir at the suggestion of the feeble, much-diluted stuff that is too often put into children's hands.

'Playing at 'History

Children have other ways of expressing the conceptions that fill them when they are duly fed. They play at history lessons, dress up, make tableaux, act scenes; or they have a stage, and their dolls act, while they paint the scenery and speak the speeches. There is no end to the modes of expression children find when there is anything in them to express.

The mistake we make is to suppose that imagination is fed by nature, or that it works on the insipid diet of children's storybooks.

Let a child have the meat he requires in his history readings, and in the literature which naturally gathers round this history, and imagination will bestir itself without any help of ours; the child will live out in detail a thousand scenes of which he only gets the merest hint.

CHAPTER 13.
FIVE TOOLS FOR TEACHING HISTORY

In this chapter I'll give you some practical tools for actually teaching history to your children.

Even if you didn't enjoy history yourself at school, or if you didn't get taught very much history at school, you can still do a good job of teaching your children history. I've got some useful tools here just for you. And if you loved history and know a heap about history, you will be able to grab the ideas here and run with them.

FIVE TOOLS FOR TEACHING HISTORY

1. HISTORY TIMELINE

WHAT IS A TIME LINE?

A time line is a very long, narrow piece of paper or card which can be mounted on a wall and which is marked like a ruler with dates throughout history. It can be used to get a visual, overall picture of historical events, and it can be added to at regular intervals, as you learn about an historical event or person.

You can start a time line when your oldest child is about eight or so. And you can keep adding to it for years and years.

I will talk more about the time line later.

2. BOOK OF CENTURIES

You can start a book of centuries when your eldest child is about eight years old. You can have a hardback book like the one on the following page, that you divide up yourself.

An advantage is that the book looks good and is neat and orderly.

A disadvantage is that you are restricted in the number of

A hardcover notebook used to create a book of centuries.

pages so it's hard to add or remove pages or have small items attached in the book.

Or you can have loose leaf pages in a ring binder or lever arch file.

If you go for loose-leaf style book then you will need to print pages for the folder which will be used for recording dates. You can print these pages in a different colour so that they are easily found in the folder as the folder starts to fill with various pieces of work that your child will do.

You need to make a page for each century. Put the century number at the top of the page. Use the markers down the left-hand side of the page to mark 25 years. And then your child can add people to the appropriate page, indicating the length of their life by a line.

As well as the century pages you will have other pages of work done on particular subjects or people.

You can downoad a book of centuries from -
http://charlottemasonmadeeasy.com/bookbonus

3. HISTORICAL NOVELS

Historical novels can never replace teaching history, but they can add richness and depth to learning. Some good authors to look out for are:

- Cynthia Harnett. She is definitely my favourite children's historical author. And my favourite novel from her books has to be The Load of Unicorn
- Rosemary Sutcliff is a great historical novelist for children and teens
- Geoffrey Trease
- Barbara Willard

Some other historical novels my children and I have read and loved are:

Adam of the Road By Janet Gray.

Adam of the Road is set in thirteenth century England and tells the fictional story of Adam Quartermayne, son of Roger the minstrel. It begins at St Alban's abbey with Adam waiting for his father to return from France where he has been studying. Roger arrives with his new employers, the de Lisles, and takes Adam and Adam's dog, Nick away with him. For a few happy months

Roger, Adam and Nick travel the road together. However, when catastrophe strikes, Adam is left alone and penniless to make his way as best he can, searching for his lost family. Janet Gray narrates his adventures with amazing precision and historical accuracy and lends a touch of drama and flair to an already unique story of what life would be like for a young boy alone in 1294. This book was first published in 1942 and was the winner of the Newbery Medal. This is a longer read (317 pages) for ages 9 +.

The Night Journey by Kathryn Lasky.

Just over a hundred years ago in Tsarist Russia, Jews were being massacred for absolutely no reason other than the simple fact that the victims were Jews. Young Jewish men were forced to join and fight in the same army that was ruthlessly killing their families. So when Great Nana Sashie begins to tell Rachel about how, at the age of nine, she escaped from these troubled circumstances with her family, Rachel cannot help but listen. The Night Journey is a National Jewish Book Award Winner. It is a very intense novel and so I recommend it only for mature 11 year olds and up.

SOME BOOKS SET DURING WW2:

The Endless Steppe by Esther Hauzig.

A young Polish girl, her mother, and her grandmother, taken prisoners by the Russians during World War II and shipped to a forced-labour camp in a remote, impoverished Siberian village.

Number the Stars by Lois Lowry.

A story set in the time of the heroic evacuation of Jews from Nazi-held Denmark by the Danish Resistance, population and police.

When Hitler Stole Pink Rabbit by Judith Kerr.

Partly autobiographical, this is first of the internationally acclaimed trilogy by Judith Kerr telling the unforgettable story of a Jewish family fleeing from Germany at the start of the Second World War.

The Wooden Horse by Eric Williams –

(Junior version) A classic escape-and-evasion story about some RAF officers who escaped from a German POW camp. First published 1949.

The Silver Sword by Ian Serraillier.
Tells the story of some children travelling across Europe during WWII in the hope of being reunited with their parents.

4. READING GOOD BOOKS

You will need to find books on the subject of what you or your child is interested in. I have found that Reader's Digest books are good for history, and National Geographic magazines are useful for historical information. The hard part will be getting issues that have articles of particular interest to what your child is learning about. But on the other hand, you can always base your interests and studies around what is available, rather than going to extreme lengths to get a special topic or issue.

Try to find something written at the time of the history that you are studying; remember Charlotte Mason said that she thought that was the best sort of reference book.

One style of teaching history is to look at social history, or you can memorise dates and events. Or you can look at people of the time. Greenleaf Guides focus on famous people to teach about the time period.

5. VISITS ...

... to local museums or outdoor sites of historical significance.

These trips and visits can be great fun and as varied and interesting as you like.

I live in a country with a comparatively small amount of history compared to other countries. The city I live near didn't even exist a couple of hundred years ago. But we still had a wonderful time exploring Auckland and finding out about its history. I bought a book called "*Walking Historic Auckland*" and every week or two for several months, we would pack a picnic, take drawing books, pencils and backpacks and drive to a spot or catch the ferry from the North Shore to the city. We often took our dog with us, and we walked, looked, read our history guide book and drew.

At the end of the project one of my children produced a beautiful display for the local 'Homeschoolers' History Fair'.

SUMMARY

In this chapter you have learned five tools for teaching history.

- A history time line
- A book of centuries
- Historical novels
- Reading good books
- Trips to museums or outdoor sites of historical significance

ASSIGNMENT

This chapter's assignment is fun: take time to enjoy browsing through history books, consider which books you might like to use with your children. Do some research and make a short list. See what's available in your local library or your home book shelf. Decide if you want to buy any books to start or add to your collection.

And here is a recommended piece of Charlotte Mason's work to read.

Volume 6, pages 169 – 180. In this passage, Charlotte Mason is referring to teaching older children.

SUPPLEMENT

Volume 6, page 169
(a) HISTORY

I have already spoken of history as a vital part of education and have cited the counsel of Montaigne that the teacher 'shall by the help of histories inform himself of the worthiest minds that were in the best ages.'

To us in particular who are living in one of the great epochs of history it is necessary to know something of what has gone before in order to think justly of what is occurring to-day. The League of Nations, for example, has reminded us not only of the Congress of Vienna but of the several Treaties of Perpetual Peace which have marked the history of Europe.—It is still true that,—

"Things done without example, in their issue Are to be feared. Have you a precedent Of this commission?" (Henry VIII.)

We applaud the bluff King's wisdom and look uneasily for precedents for the war and the peace and the depressing anxieties that have come in their train.

We are conscious of a lack of sound judgment in ourselves to decide upon the questions that have come before us and are aware that nothing would give us more confidence than a pretty wide acquaintance with history.

The more educated among our 'Dominion' cousins complain that their young people have no background of history and as a consequence' we are the people' is their master thought; they would face even the loss of Westminster Abbey without a qualm. What is it to them where great events have happened, great persons lived and moved?

And, alas, this indifference to history is not confined to the Dominions; young people at home are equally indifferent, nor have their elders such stores of interest and information as should quicken children with the knowledge that always and everywhere there have been great parts to play and almost always great men to play those parts: that any day it may come to anyone to do some service of historical moment to the country.

It is not too much to say that a rational well-considered patriotism depends on a pretty copious reading of history, and with this rational patriotism we desire our young people shall be informed rather than with the jingoism of the emotional patriot.

If there is but little knowledge of history amongst us, no doubt our schools are in fault. Teachers will plead that there is no time save for a sketchy knowledge of English history given in a course of lectures of which the pupils take notes and work up reports.

Most of us know how unsatisfying is such a course however entertaining. Not even Thackeray could introduce the stuff of knowledge into his lectures on The Four Georges. Our knowledge of history should give us something more than impressions and opinions, but, alas, the lack of time is a real difficulty.

Now the method I am advocating has this advantage; it multiplies time. Each school period is quadrupled in time value and we find that we get through a surprising amount of history in a thorough way, in about the same time that in most schools affords no more than a skeleton of English History only.

We know that young people are enormously interested in the subject and give concentrated attention if we give them the right books. We are aware that our own discursive talk is usually a waste of time and a strain on the scholars' attention, so we (of the P.N.E.U.) [Parents' National Education Union, an organisation set up to encourage and teach Miss Mason's philosophy of education] confine ourselves to affording two things,—knowledge, and a keen sympathy in the interest roused by that knowledge. It is our part to see that every child knows and can tell, whether by way of oral narrative or written essay. In this way an unusual amount of ground is covered with such certainty that no revision is required for the examination at the end of the term.

A single reading is a condition insisted upon because a naturally desultory habit of mind leads us all to put off the effort of attention as long as a second or third chance of coping with our subject is to be hoped for. It is, however, a mistake to speak of the 'effort of attention.'

Complete and entire attention is a natural function which requires no effort and causes no fatigue; the anxious labour of mind of which we are at times aware comes when attention wanders and has again to be brought to the point; but the concentration at which most teachers aim is an innate provision for education and is not the result of training or effort.

Our concern is to afford matter of a sufficiently literary character, together with the certainty that no second or third opportunity for knowing a given lesson will be allowed.

The personality of the teacher is no doubt of much value but perhaps this value is intellectual rather than emotional—The perception of the teacher is keenly interested, that his mind and their minds are working in harmony is a wonderful incentive to young scholars; but the sympathetic teacher who believes that to attend is a strain, who makes allowance for the hundred wandering fancies that beset a child—whom he has at last to pull up with effort, tiring to teacher and pupil—hinders in his good-natured efforts to help.

The child of six in 1B has, not stories from English History, but a definite quantity of consecutive reading, say, forty pages in a term, from a well-written, well-considered, large volume which is also well-illustrated.

Children cannot of course themselves read a book which is by no means written down to the 'child's level' so the teacher reads and the children 'tell' paragraph by paragraph, passage by passage. The teacher does not talk much and is careful never to interrupt a child who is called upon to 'tell.' The first efforts may be stumbling but presently the children get into their 'stride' and 'tell' a passage at length with surprising fluency.

The teacher probably allows other children to correct any faults in the telling when it is over. The teacher's own really difficult part is to keep up sympathetic interest by look and occasional word, by remarks upon a passage that has been narrated, by occasionally shewing pictures, and so on. But she will bear in mind that the child of six has begun the serious business of his education, that it does not matter much whether he understands this word or that, but that it matters a great deal that he should learn to deal directly with books.

Whatever a child or grown-up person can tell, that we may be sure he knows, and what he cannot tell, he does not know. Possibly this practice of 'telling' was more used in the sixteenth and seventeenth centuries than it is now. We remember how three gentlemen meet in Henry VIII and one who has just come out of the Abbey from witnessing the coronation of Anne Boleyn is asked to tell the others about it, which he does with the vividness and accuracy we obtain from children. In this case no doubt the 'telling' was a stage device, but would it have been adopted if such narration were not commonly practised? Even in our own day a good raconteur is a welcome guest; and a generation or two ago the art was studied as a part of gentlemanly equipment. The objection occurs that such a social accomplishment is unnecessary for children and is a mere exercise of memory.

Now a passage to be memorised requires much conning, much repetition, and meanwhile the learners are 'thinking' about other matters, that is, the mind is not at work in the act of memorising. To read a passage with full attention and to tell it afterwards has a curiously different effect. M. Bergson makes the happy distinction between word memory and mind memory, which, once the force of it is realised, should bring about sweeping changes in our methods of education.

Trusting to mind memory we visualise the scene, are convinced by the arguments, take pleasure in the turn the sentences and frame our own upon them; in that particular passage or chapter has been received us and become a part of us just as literally as was yesterday's dinner; nay, more so, for yesterday's dinner is little account tomorrow; but several months, perhaps hence, we shall be able to narrate the passage, we so to say, consumed and grown upon with all the vividness, detail and accuracy of the first telling.

All powers of the mind which we call faculties have brought into play in dealing with the, intellectual matter thus afforded; so we may not ask questions to help the child to reason, paint fancy pictures to help him to imagine, draw out moral lessons to quicken his conscience. These things take place as involuntarily as processes of digestion.

Children of seven are promoted to Form 1A in which they remain for a couple of years. They read from the same capital book, Mrs. Marshall's Our Island Story, and about the same number of pages in a term; but while the readings in 1B are confined to the first third of the book embodying the simpler and more direct histories, those in 1A go on to the end of the volume and children learn at any rate to love English history. "I'd a lot sooner have history than my dinner," said a sturdy boy of seven by no means inclined to neglect his dinner.

In 1A the history is amplified and illustrated by short

biographies of persons connected with the period studied, Lord Clive, Nelson, etc.; and Mrs. Frewen Lord's delightful Tales from Westminster Abbey and from St. Paul's help the children immensely in individualising their heroes. It is good to hear them 'tell' of Franklin, Nelson, Howard, Shaftesbury, and their delight in visiting the monuments is very great. One would not think that Donne would greatly interest children but the excitement of a small party in noticing the marks of the Great Fire still to be seen on his monument was illuminating to lookers-on.

Possibly there is no sounder method of inculcating a sane and serviceable patriotism than this of making children familiar with the monuments of the great event if they have not the opportunity to see them. Form II (ages 9 to 12) have a more considerable historical programme which they cover with ease and enjoyment. They use a more difficult book than in IA, an interesting and well-written history of England of which they read some fifty pages or so in a term. IIA read in addition and by way of illustration the chapters dealing with the social life of the period in a volume, treating of social life in England.

We introduce children as early as possible to the contemporary history of other countries as the study of English history alone is apt to lead to a certain insular and arrogant habit of mind.

Naturally we begin with French history and both divisions read from the First History of France, very well written, the chapters contemporary with the English history they are reading. The readiness with which children write or tell of Richelieu, Colbert, Bayard, justifies us in this early introduction of foreign history and the lucidity and clearness with which the story is told in the book they use results on the part of the children in such a knowledge of the history of France as throws light on that of their own country and certainly gives them the sense that history was progressing everywhere much as it was at home during the period they are reading about.

The study of ancient history which cannot be contemporaneous we approach through a chronologically-arranged book about the British Museum (written for the scholars of the P.U.S. by the late Mrs. W. Epps who had the delightful gift of realising the progress of the ages as represented in our great national storehouse). I have already instanced a child's visit to the Parthenon Room and her eager identification of what she saw with what she had read, and that will serve to indicate the sort of key to ancient history afforded by this valuable book. Miss G. M. Bernau has added to the value of these studies by producing a Book of Centuries' in which children draw such illustrations as they come across of objects of domestic use, of art, etc., connected with the century they are reading about.

This slight study of the British Museum we find very valuable; whether the children have or have not the opportunity of visiting the Museum itself, they have the hope of doing so, and, besides, their minds are awakened to the treasures of local museums.

In Form III children continue the same history of England as in II, the same French history and the same British Museum Book, going on with their 'Book of Centuries.' To this they add about twenty to thirty pages a term from a little book on Indian History, a subject which interests them greatly.

Slight studies of the history of other parts of the British Empire are included under 'Geography.'

In Form IV the children are promoted to Gardiner's Student's History of England, clear and able, but somewhat stiffer than that they have hitherto been engaged upon, together with Mr. and Mrs. Quennell's History of Everyday Things in England (which is used in Form III also). Form IV is introduced to outlines of European history. The British Museum for Children and 'Book of Centuries are continued.

It is as teachers know a matter of extreme difficulty to find the exactly right book for children's reading in each subject and for some years we have been regretting the fact that Lord's very delightful Modern Europe 1 has been out of print.

The history studies of Forms V and VI (ages 15 to 18) are more advanced and more copious and depend for illustration upon readings in the literature of the period. Green's Shorter History of the English People is the textbook in English history, amplified, for example, by Macaulay's Essays on Frederick the Great and the Austrian Succession, on Pitt and Clive. For the same period we use an American history of Western Europe and a very admirable history of France, well-translated from the original of M. Duruy. Possibly Madame de Staël's L'Allemagne or some other historical work of equal calibre may occur in their reading of French.

It is not possible to continue the study of Greek and Roman

history in detail but an admirably written survey informed with enthusiasm is afforded by Professor de Burgh's The Legacy of the Ancient World. The pupils make history charts for every hundred years on the plan either adapted or invented by the late Miss Beale of Cheltenham, a square ruled into a hundred spaces ten in each direction with the symbol in each square showing an event which lends itself to illustration during that particular ten years. Thus crossed battle axes represent a war.

The geographical aspects of history fall under 'Geography' as a subject. This course of historical reading is valued exceedingly by young people as affording a knowledge of the past that bears upon and illuminates the present. The writer recollects meeting a brilliant group of Oxford undergraduates, keen and full of interest, but lamentably ignorant, who said, "We want to know something about history. What do you advise us to read? We know nothing."

Perhaps no youth should go to College without some such rudimentary course of English, European, and, especially, French history, as is afforded by the programmes 1. Such a general survey should precede any special course and should be required before the more academic studies designed to prepare students for 'research work.'

It will be observed that the work throughout the Forms is always chronologically progressive. The young student rarely goes over old ground; but should it happen that the whole school has arrived at the end of 1920, say, and there is nothing for it but to begin again, the books studied throw new light and bring the young students into line with modern research.

But any sketch of the history teaching in Forms V and VI in a given period depends upon a notice of the 'literature' set; for plays, novels, essays, 'lives,' poems, are all pressed into service and where it is possible, the architecture, painting, etc., which the period produced.

Thus questions such as the following on a term's work both test and record the reading of the term,—

- "Describe the condition of (a) the clergy, (b) the army, (c) the navy, (d) the general public in and about 1685."
- "Trace the rise of Prussia before Frederick the Great."

- "What theories of government were held by Louis XIV? Give some account of his great ministers."
- "Describe the rise of Russia and its condition at the opening of the eighteenth century." "
- Suppose Evelyn (Form VI) or Pepys (Form V) in counsel at the League of Nations, write his diary for three days."
- "Sketch the character and manners of Addison. How does he appear in Esmond?"

It is a great thing to possess a pageant of history in the background of one's thoughts. We may not be able to recall this or that circumstance, but, 'the imagination is warmed'; we know that there is a great deal to be said on both sides of every question and are saved from crudities in opinion and rashness in action.

The present becomes enriched for us with the wealth of all that has gone before.

Perhaps the gravest defect in school curricula is that they fail to give a comprehensive, intelligent and interesting introduction to history. To leave off or even to begin with the history of our own country is fatal. We can not live sanely unless we know that other peoples are as we are with a difference, that their history is as ours, with a difference, that they too have been represented by their poets and their artists, that they too have their literature and their national life. We have been asleep and our awaking is rather terrible. The people whom we have not taught, rise upon us in their ignorance and 'the rabble,'—

"As the world were now but to begin Antiquity forgot, custom not known. They cry,—'Choose we!'" (Hamlet.)

Heaven help their choice for choosing is indeed with them, and little do they know of those two ratifiers and props of every present word and action, Antiquity and Custom!

It is never too late to mend but we may not delay to offer such a liberal and generous diet of History to every child in the country as shall give weight to his decisions, consideration to his actions and stability to his conduct. that stability, the lack of which has plunged us into many a stormy sea of unrest.

It is to be noted that 'stability' is the mark of the educated classes. When we reflect upon the disturbance of the national life by labour unrest and again, upon the fact that political and *social power is passing into the hands of the majority, that is of the labouring classes, we cannot but feel that there is a divine fitness, a providential adaptation in the circumstance that the infinite educability of persons of all classes should be disclosed to us as a nation at a time when an emotional and ignorant labouring class is a peculiar danger. I am not sure that the education implied in the old symbol of the ladder does make for national tranquillity.*

It is right that equal opportunity of being first should be afforded to all but that is no new thing. Our history is punctuated by men who have risen, and the Roman Church has largely founded herself as has the Chinese Empire upon this doctrine .of equal opportunity. But let us remember that the men who climb are apt to be uneasy members of society; the desire for knowledge for its own sake, on the other hand, finds satisfaction in knowledge itself.

The young men see visions; the hardships of daily life are ameliorated, and while an alert and informed mind leads to decency and propriety of living it does not lead to the restless desire to subvert society for the sake of the chances offered by a general upheaval. Wordsworth is right:—

If rightly trained and bred Humanity is humble."

We live in times critical for everybody but eminently critical for teachers because it rests with them to decide whether personal or general good should be aimed at, whether education shall be merely a means of getting on or a means of general progress towards high thinking and plain living and therefore an instrument of the greatest national good.

CHAPTER 14.
HOW TO MAKE YOUR OWN TIMELINE

WHAT IS A TIME LINE?

A timeline is a long chart, which can be mounted on a wall and which shows dates throughout history. It gives a great, visual, overall picture of historical events, and it can be added to at regular intervals over several years, as you teach (or learn) about an historical event or person.

MAKING A SIMPLE TIMELINE

Because the timeline will span about 6000 years, you will see that the space between centuries is very small. Don't worry about this; it does work. I will show you how you can fit lots of information into the space.

LIST OF MATERIALS :

- 3-metre strip of paper. (A piece of till roll – the paper roll used in cash registers - is good.)
- A4 sheets of different coloured card.
- 2 indelible marker pens,
- Needle and thread.

TO MAKE THE TIME LINE:

First mark your time line using an indelible, non-fade felt marker pen by marking off every 5 centimetres. Each five centimetres will be the equivalent of 100 years of time on the time line. Each decade can be marked off in half centimetre sections.

Write in the 100 years. I recommend that you write them in with pencil first, so that if you make a mistake you can sort it out easily. (This is the voice of experience speaking – I made more than two attempts at marking our timeline because I kept getting distracted and writing the wrong numbers) Then you just write over the top in indelible pen.

Because there is very little information about early history you will need to pick a date to start your time line. I started my time line at 4000BC as that ensured that every firm date in history would be included. All history before recorded history is 'prehistory'.

Mark every hundred years going down from 4000BC to the birth of Christ. Change the colour of your pen and start marking the centuries going up to 2000AD.

If you want to strengthen your timeline you can glue your long white strip of paper to a stronger background paper, giving a 2cm or 3 cm border.

Your time line is now ready to mount on the wall. The best height for this is about eye-level height for your children but high enough to keep it protected from inquisitive younger children. Because not many houses have a clear three metre (ten foot) strip of wall at child-eye-level some people use the stairway for the time line.

Or you might choose to put the time line high up on the wall but explain to the children that this is a compromise.

Or you might choose to make a timeline like a very large poster with rows of lines.

Or you might choose to do only the past 2000 years.

Whatever you decide to do, you will need to talk to your children about it and help them to read it and to put in additions when necessary.

TO MAKE THE TIME CARDS:

Cut the card into 5x5cm squares.

Look at the colour key the end of these instructions and start preparing the cards to add to the time line. As your children study historical figures or events in Bible studies, story reading, any other studies or any other time, they can add them to the chart. The children will make the timecards themselves and write their own version of events.

Keep the cards in a zip lock bag or small box with the needle and the pens so that you can add more cards to your timeline quite easily when you want to.

Write on your card the basic fact and a date on one side.

For example, the time line in my house had a card about Mt Vesuvius erupting. The card read: *Mt Vesuvius erupted, 79AD*. Then on the reverse my child had written more detail: *In August 79AD Mt Vesuvius erupted covering Herculaneum with 20 metres of ash and lava. The nearby city of Pompeii was also covered but with only 4 metres of ash and rock. Both Pompeii and Herculaneum are being excavated now.*

Another example from our timeline looked like this: on one side it read *Jane Austen - b. 1775. d. 1817.* The other side read *- Jane Austen wrote many books including Pride and Prejudice and Northanger Abbey. She never married and was devoted to her sister.*

Mount the time cards on the time line using the needle and thread. Sew through a corner of the card (not too close to the edge) and then attach the card to the time line using the needle. Have the card hanging one or two centimetres under the time line. To accommodate several cards in a small time span make the card threads different lengths so that some cards hang lower than others.

Tip: You will find that as time goes on you will have heaps of cards to put on the time line from the Middle Ages onwards. In fact there is very little history to record from pre-Roman times. You may wish to start your time line with the Romans or with the birth of Jesus. This will make your time line shorter if you don't have a lot of space.

TIME CARD COLOUR KEY

Red	Kings, Queens and Statesmen.
Blue	Artists, Musicians and Writers.
Green	Explorers and Inventors.
White	Men of God.
Yellow	Events.
Orange	Your family.

USEFUL DATES

These dates might be useful to you in starting your time line.

Sparta	circa 2002BC
Ancient Greece	circa 2000BC
First Egyptian Dynasty starts	circa 2000BC
Sundials used in Egypt	circa 1500BC
King Tutankhamen dies	1358BC
King David	1055BC
Elisha	850BC
First Olympic Games	776BC
Founding of Rome	753BC
Daniel is born	606BC
Sugar was discovered	325BC
Archimedes is born	287BC
JESUS, SON OF GOD is born	7BC
(The world is never the same again)	
Mt Vesuvius erupts	79AD
Viking raids start	790AD
Columbus is born	1451AD
Michelangelo is born	1475AD
Henry VIII is born	1491AD
Elizabeth I is born	1533AD
Shakespeare is born	1564AD
Tasman discovers NZ	1642AD
John Wesley is born	1703AD
Captain Cook is born	1728AD
Start of Am. War of Independence	1775AD
French Revolution	1789AD
Treaty of Waitangi	1841AD
Start of WW1	1914AD
Start of WW2	1939AD

Add your own name and family dates.
ENJOY!

A LAST WORD

Now that you have completed this book you will hopefully want to continue applying what you have learned with your family. This book has majored on a few of Charlotte Mason's philosophies like ideas, living books, habits, nature walks, science and history.

Hopefully, you will want to continue to read Charlotte Mason's work and I have a couple of hints to help you do that.

HELPFUL HINTS

When you are reading your copy of Charlotte Mason, it helps to read with a pencil in your hand. Make sure you mark:

- The date at the top of each page as you read it. If you are reading it for the second time, put the date again, and so on. This way you will see what you have read, and which passages you have read more than once.
- Use your pencil to write notes and comments in the margin.
- Underline parts that you find very helpful or interesting.
- Make use of smiley faces, questions marks, exclamations, post-it notes, etc. These will remind you of the thoughts and opinions you had while reading, when you do go back and re-read.

If you would like to write to me about this book, about homeschooling or about Charlotte Mason's ideas and philosophies I would love to hear from you. Write to me stephanie@charlottemasonmadeeasy.com

ABOUT THE AUTHOR

Stephanie Walmsley is a teacher by profession, with classroom teaching experience in New Zealand and England. She and her husband, Philip, started officially homeschooling their five children in January 1985. The older two had a couple of spells in school; the younger three never went to school.

She worked as a volunteer for over twenty years, supporting mothers in their mothering and homeschooling. Then in 2002 she started writing and conducting courses for homeschooling parents because she saw a need for good, professional, homeschool help available from someone who has 'walked the talk'.

She has written a series of online courses for homeschooling mothers, and also has eBooks and study guides available.

Her passion is to support parents with their children and especially in their home education.

Visit Stephanie at www.charlottemasonmadeeasy.com

Lightning Source UK Ltd.
Milton Keynes UK
UKHW041355250221
379328UK00003B/895